*MARY LYON OF PUTNAM'S HILL

A biography by EVELYN I. BANNING

Mary Lyon
OF PUTNAM'S HILL

THE VANGUARD PRESS, INC. *New York*

Copyright, ©, 1965, by Evelyn I. Banning

Published simultaneously in Canada by the
Copp, Clark Publishing Company, Ltd., Toronto

No portion of this book may be reprinted in any
form without the written permission of the publisher,
except by a reviewer who may wish to quote brief
passages in connection with a review for a newspaper,
magazine, radio or television.

Manufactured in the United States of America by
H. Wolff, New York, N.Y.

Library of Congress Catalogue Card Number: 65-10683

To Evelyn Rose Robinson

INTRODUCTION

All the members of Mary Lyon's family, those of the White family of Ashfield, Massachusetts, and all the teachers named in this biography of Mary Lyon are authentic. The only fictitious characters are minor ones whose identity could not be determined from the records. They do, however, represent families and names typical of Massachusetts in the nineteenth century.

Some incidents have been imagined for the purpose of the story, but the biography is basically true. The author has kept in mind the background and the character of the real people.

In my research, I drew heavily upon town records in the localities in which Mary Lyon lived, studied, and taught, and I examined the accounts of the schools with which she was in any way associated, all of which I visited. Many of the personal details were obtained from letters, newspapers, and school catalogues. My chief source of published material was Edward Hitchcock's *Memoir of Mary Lyon*.

ACKNOWLEDGMENTS

Many people have helped me, and to all of them I am truly grateful. I would like to thank in particular the librarians who assisted me, especially Miss Flora B. Ludington, librarian of Mount Holyoke College, who gave me access to Mary Lyon's personal letters and documents; Miss Edith O. Hall, librarian of the Derry Public Library, Derry, New Hampshire; and Miss Laura Louise Monnier, formerly cataloguer of the Wheaton College Library.

Miss Ruth Berchard of the Buckland Historical Society was of great help, as were Mrs. Mary Priscilla Howes of Ashfield, who lent me invaluable references; Mrs. John T. Litch, who shared with me her knowledge and recollections of Byfield Seminary; and Mrs. James Newton, curator of Whipple House, Ipswich, Massachusetts. I am also indebted to the late Miss Jennie Copeland for the use of material on the Wheaton family and her unpublished manuscript of the life of Judge Wheaton.

Mr. Galen Johnson of East Buckland willingly gave his

time to answer many questions about the early life on Putnam's Hill and to recall stories of his Grandmother Ware, who had been a schoolmate of Mary Lyon in the district school in Hog Hollow. My friend, Miss Evelyn Rose Robinson, to whom this book is dedicated, climbed Putnam's Hill with me, went with me on many trips in New England and New York, read manuscript, and listened to and encouraged me.

E. I. B.

CONTENTS

1
THE MOUNTAIN HOME *15*

2
SCHOOL IN ASHFIELD *23*

3
THE EMPTY FARMHOUSE *31*

4
GROWING UP *42*

5
SOME BEGINNINGS *48*

6
A LOCKET FOR LOVE *56*

7
A NEW HOME *64*

8
A TURNING POINT *73*

9
THE MORNING COACH
FROM ALBANY *81*

10
A LOCKET RETURNED *87*

11
A GREEN VELVET BAG *94*

12
THE MAJESTIC HUDSON *105*

13
THE MARQUIS DE LAFAYETTE *114*

14
ON A CRUSADE *121*

15
A TRIP WEST *129*

16
BREAKING GROUND AT
SOUTH HADLEY *140*

17
TROUBLED TIMES *151*

18
HAPPY DAYS *161*

19
A TENTH ANNIVERSARY *172*

20
A CHAIN OF IVY *179*

SELECTED LIST OF AUTHORITIES *187*

*MARY LYON OF PUTNAM'S HILL

I

THE MOUNTAIN HOME

Mary Mason Lyon could hear the crackle of the logs in the kitchen fireplace. She listened for the familiar sounds of the morning: her mother preparing the corn-meal mush in the wooden porringer and her brother Aaron bringing the day's supply of wood from the shed. Then she heard the grating of the barn door and knew Aaron was on his way to feed the sheep and milk the cows. It was time to get up.

From the bedroom window Mary looked out at the pasture, white with a fresh fall of snow. Usually from that small north window she could see the pasture fence and the gate leading into the orchard. But snow had fallen most of the night and the fence was all but hidden from sight by the heavy drifts.

"I suppose," sighed Mary, "we'll not be going to the village this morning."

She hadn't counted on the heavy snowfall. She looked

✻

again at the trees outlined sharply against the blue of the sky, her lips moving silently.

Shivering, she closed the window and crossed the bare floor to waken Rosina.

Tossing her nightgown onto the nearest chair, she pulled on a flannel petticoat and dress, a brown hand-me-down from her mother. Then she brushed back the red hair from her shoulders.

"Don't keep Ma waiting," she called to Rosina as she closed the bedroom door.

Quickly she hurried down the steep flight of stairs that led into the kitchen. It was a small room, bare but comfortable. A spinning wheel and hand loom filled one corner, and a hutch table and six ladder-back chairs were the only other pieces of furniture in the room. The dishes, mostly wooden bowls and plates, were on the open corner shelves.

"Morning, Ma," said Mary. She warmed her hands in front of the fireplace and then took the large bowl of mush over to the table and set it down.

"Come on, Freelove. Time to eat," she called to her youngest sister, who sat on the floor quietly hooking her shoes. Freelove was four and a half, a slight, shy child. Her frequent illnesses worried the family, and Mary took care of her at times when her mother was busy with other tasks.

Aaron arrived with a pail of milk and the family sat down to breakfast.

"Guess we can't go to the village, Ma," Mary complained. "I wish the snow had held off for another day."

She knew there would be no trip to Jones' country store in Buckland, with its rows and rows of glass jars filled with "goodies," horehound candies and ginger; nor would there be a visit with Uncle Nate and the family. But there was still the weaving to do, and she might be able to finish the cloth for the girls' new school dresses.

"And maybe time enough to dye some of it," thought Mary, who, at nine, had little time to play.

"I know, Mary, there's plenty to be done indoors," said Mrs. Lyon, sounding as cross as Mary felt.

"May I—may I work at the loom?" Mary asked with slight hesitation. She hoped her mother wouldn't ask her to spin. She didn't mind carding the wool and rolling it between the smooth backs of the wooden paddles, but she was all thumbs when it came to spinning. And she felt embarrassed whenever her mother sang:

*"It's not in the wheel, it's not in the band;
It's in the girl who takes it in hand."*

"May I, Ma?" Mary persisted.

"Have you finished carding the wool that Aaron brought in from the shed?" That was one thing about her mother—no new task was to be started until the old one had been finished.

"Not all of it, Ma, but couldn't Rosina card the rest while I weave?"

"Sure, Ma," Rosina answered for her, "sure, I'll card. And Freelove can help, can't you, 'Love?"

"Sure can, Rosie, sure can," agreed Freelove, a veritable mimic.

After the breakfast dishes had been put away, Mary helped with the baking and the cooking while the girls sat and carded the wool. There was bread to bake almost every day, but on Saturdays Mary and her mother cooked the meat and the

✳

puddings, for in the Lyon family no work was done on Sunday.

At last the bread had been set for baking in the brick oven and, brushing the flour off the front of her dress, Mary sat down on the long bench at the four-harness loom and confidently tightened the threads. Better than almost anything else she liked to weave. The weaving went easily, back and forth with the shuttle, and up and down with her feet on the treadles—one and three, two and four.

In no time at all the cloth would be long enough and then there would be the dyeing. Last fall Mary had gathered peach leaves, which she had carefully stored in the shed. Some of the leaves she had found in an old orchard near the farmhouse. The farm on which the Lyons had lived for many years was on Putnam's Hill in East Buckland, fifteen miles west of Deerfield in western Massachusetts.

It was America just after the turn of the century. Thomas Jefferson, the third president, had just purchased the Louisiana Territory for the United States. America had extended from the Mississippi to the Rockies.

Mary lived far removed, however, from the busy life of a city. The Lyon farm was located on the side of Putnam's Hill, a good mile from Buckland Center and a long walk to the nearest neighbor. She often roamed the hill in back of her house. "Just like your father used to," her mother would say.

From the top of Putnam's Hill she could look down on Buckland Center and Clesson's River, and on a clear day she could even see Mount Holyoke standing like a sentinel on the bank of the Connecticut River. Years later she used to say, "The mountains were my first teachers. They taught me patience."

On these hills she collected specimens of plants and flowers; "weeds," her mother called them. And from the brook that ran along the lower meadow she had found chocolate drops, white violets, and the delicate star flower. These, with many others, she classified, pressed, and placed high on the rafters in the upstairs loft out of the way of prying sisters.

"The peach leaves will dye a sort of yellowish color. How would that be, Ma?" Mary's blue eyes brightened. "Could we try them?"

Mary's dresses had always been dyed blue or brown, indigo blue for Sunday, and brown for everyday wear.

"You and your weeds, Mary. How do you find out about these plants?"

"It's just that I'm interested, Ma. One of Pa's old books told about the peach leaves—" She had no sooner mentioned her father than she wished she hadn't. It always brought a tight look to her mother's face, though four winters had come and gone since his death in December of 1802. She hastened to add, "I wanted to try smartweed—Mrs. Ware says it makes a reddish shade—but I couldn't find enough plants to brew."

"I don't see anything wrong with brown for school," Mrs. Lyon said, glancing up from her work.

"But could we try even one dyeing, Ma?" urged Mary.

"I'd like that too," added Rosina, nodding vigorously. "May we, Ma?"

"May we, Ma?" repeated Freelove, her face a slight pout but her eyes large with excitement.

"Why, girls, we would have a mess, peach stains all over the place. And what is wrong with brown? Don't you like the dress you have on, Mary?"

✱

"Yes, Ma, I like it, but I don't go to school."

Mary hadn't been to school for almost three years. It made no difference to her what color she wore, but with Rosina it was different. She had so wanted a bright dress.

Rosina was seven, two years younger than Mary and not so tall or so large of frame; she was an exceptionally attractive girl with delicate features like her mother's.

"What about taking some of the wool to Mr. Pomeroy's mill? He could dye it red, the way he did the flannel last time," Mary said.

"That would mean an extra trip for your brother." But Mrs. Lyon looked thoughtful. Mary held her breath, for her mother seldom changed her mind.

"Aaron won't mind, Ma. Could we?" Mary pleaded.

"I guess we might," she said.

Rosina clapped her hands. "Think of it, Freelove, red dresses!" Then, holding onto Freelove, she danced and skipped around the room.

"I'll make a few more pounds of butter," Mary thought.

Mr. Jones had paid twelve cents a pound for butter the last time. Mary figured that five pounds would easily pay for dyeing cloth for at least one dress. Rosina should have her new dress in time for the next school term.

At times like this, Mary recalled her school days with a kind of longing. She'd like to study again, but she was the oldest girl at home now and her mother depended on her help. Her three older sisters were no longer at home. Electa, twenty-one years old, and Jemima, nineteen, were teaching school and boarding out. Lovina, almost thirteen years old, had gone to "live in" and work for the Woodwards.

Although Mary knew how to read and write, and could

THE MOUNTAIN HOME

figure a little, there was much, much more to learn. "Maybe later," her mother always said.

Mary remembered—or thought she remembered—the story the family often told about the first time she asked to go to school. She was almost four years old—would be in a few months, on February 28, 1801.

"You are too little," her mother had answered sharply. "You can go next spring. Your sisters didn't go until they were six, and Aaron stayed home until he was seven."

Parents, not the law, decided when children could go to school at this time, and in country districts in early Massachusetts four-year-olds were seldom welcome with the older boys and girls.

"But I want to go, Ma," Mary had cried. "Please, Ma. And I can read. Ask Pa or Electa."

"I said next year, Mary." It did no good to plead with her mother.

So Mary had gone over to her father, who was rocking baby Rosine.

"I'm a big girl, Pa. Why can't I go?"

"Your mother said 'no,' and it's a long walk, Mary."

"I can walk fast, Pa. Honest I can." Mary reached out and took his hand from the cradle, her eyes pleading.

"But the others will get ahead of you, and you will be a nuisance."

"No, I won't, Pa. I'll be as quiet as a mouse."

Mary would not be put off. It was no use. Mr. Lyon could find no answer to satisfy Mary. It was indeed a long walk for a child not yet four—a mile down the west side of Putnam's Hill, beyond the Wares in Hog Hollow.

"If you can keep up with Aaron and the girls, you may

✱

go," he finally said. "But no tears, mind you, even if your sisters leave you at home because you're too slow. You are not to fuss, remember."

Mary had thrown her arms around her father and rushed to tell the news that she was going to "school, school, school!"

That year she had read from the *New England Primer*. In it were some poems and a number of animal pictures with a rhyme for each, an illustrated alphabet, and the Lord's Prayer. Mary memorized most of the poems and stories.

It was the same book her older sisters had used, a small volume that fit easily into her coat pocket. In the 1800's, children took their own books to school. They cost money, and the Lyon family passed them down from one child to another.

On her return each day from the district school, Mary recited her lessons to her father. Sometimes father and daughter shared the stories in the *Primer,* but more often Mary read from Webster's *American Spelling Book,* a gift from her father on her fourth birthday.

"You'll spoil that girl with all your attention," complained Mrs. Lyon. "You forget that you have four other daughters."

Then came a day in late December the following year that she would remember as long as she lived.

2

SCHOOL IN ASHFIELD

It was a cold, crisp day, that December twenty-first of 1802, and the wind blew wisps of snow around the house. Mary put on her coat and went in search of Aaron. She was frightened and unhappy. She was glad to be out of the kitchen, for she hated the smell of mustard and lard plasters. Something must be very wrong! Otherwise why had Electa left her schoolteaching in Buckland to come home?

"Where are you going?" she called to Aaron, who was harnessing old Tom. Aaron was a tall, scrawny, and rather unattractive boy of thirteen.

At the sight of Mary, he stopped for a moment. Then he fastened the reins to the side of the sleigh and gently patted the horse.

"Why, Mary, what's the matter?" he asked.

"Tell me, Aaron. Is . . . is Pa going to die?"

"I don't think so, Mary," said Aaron soothingly. "But he's

awful sick and I'm going to drive over to Conway for the doctor."

"Oh, Aaron, I'm so afraid—and Ma says I must go to school just the same."

"That's right. Be a good girl, Mary, and I'll be back by noon. You'll see. Pa will be all right again."

Sickness was rare in the Lyon family. Usually it was Mr. Lyon whom the neighbors called for when someone was ill. He knew a great deal about the healing power of herbs and could even set a broken bone successfully.

"Only a few weeks ago," thought Mary, "only a few weeks ago everything was so different." It had been Thanksgiving Day, and the house was full of fun and laughter. Uncle Nate and his large family had driven over from Buckland, and Electa had come home for the holiday. For dinner there had been roast pig, baked potatoes, johnnycake, and apple pie.

But best of all were the stories that Father and Uncle Nate had told—exciting tales of bears, wildcats, and Indians in Old Deerfield. They had finally talked of the famous Battle of Bennington, when as boys they had gone to Vermont and fought side by side on that sixteenth of August, 1777, with the Green Mountain Boys. Later she learned that her father had served heroically in this battle that paved the way for American independence.

Reluctantly, Mary went off to school with Lovina. At the last minute, Jemima decided not to go. School attendance was not required in those days and Jemima, now fifteen, often stayed home.

The lessons dragged on and for the first time Mary was glad to hear the closing bell.

It was nearly dark when she and Lovina reached the farmhouse. As she kicked off her heavy boots in the shed, she thought she heard a cry. Then all was silent.

"Did you hear a noise?" she asked Lovina, who was busily hanging up her wraps. At eight years of age, Lovina was the bustling, tidy one of the family. Mary found it hard to keep up with her.

"Hear what?" Lovina asked impatiently.

Mary listened. "Shh," she said. "Someone crying?"

"No, I can't hear a sound. But hurry, Mary."

Pulling off the leggings, Mary called, "Wait for me, Lovina, I'm coming." Then she brushed off the snow and threw coat, mittens, and leggings in a heap on the floor. "Wait for me," she called again.

The kitchen was empty but Mary could see the doctor, leaning against the doorjamb of the bedroom. Aaron and her sisters were standing around the big bed. She crowded in close to the bedside. Her father lay motionless.

She would never forget his pale and quiet face, nor the sight of her mother kneeling by the bed, head bowed. It was a long time before anyone spoke or moved.

Slowly her mother got up. "Close the blinds, Electa, and leave me alone." And, turning to the doctor, she said wearily, "There's nothing you can do here."

Mary fled to the upstairs bedroom, where Electa later found her huddled in a corner, sobbing. Electa picked her up and sat with her in the hide-bottomed chair. Mary buried her face in Electa's shoulder and sobbed, "He's gone. Pa's gone."

"Shh," comforted Electa. In her own sorrow, Mary was unaware of her sister's tears. She felt only a great emptiness.

From that time on, Mrs. Lyon carried the full responsibility for the family of seven, six girls and a boy. Aaron, like his father, knew every tree and rock on the place and proved to be a good farmer.

Electa, the oldest, now seventeen, went back to schoolteaching in Buckland, and within a few years Jemima left to teach in nearby Shelburne Falls and Lovina went to live with the Woodwards and help with the housework.

Then Mary was the oldest girl at home, busy from morning to night helping with the housework and looking after Freelove when she wasn't well enough to go to school with Rosina.

At times Mary worked with Aaron in the garden and orchard.

Although there was always much to do both inside and outside the farmhouse, Mary still found time to climb the hills and wander through the woods and fields around Putnam's Hill. She missed going to school, but she read the books that her sisters brought home. And she knew Webster's *American Spelling Book* and Adams' *School Geography* almost by heart.

It wasn't until the fall of 1807 that Aaron was able to persuade his mother that Mary should have a chance to go to school again.

"She could earn her keep, Ma," Aaron had explained. "The Elmers of Ashfield are looking for a hired girl, I hear. Shall I ask them if they'll take Mary?"

Mrs. Lyon hesitated. True, she had often seen Mary eagerly helping Rosina with her lessons, and no amount of scolding had ever stopped Mary from reading by candlelight in her room. Still, she didn't know how she could spare her.

Aaron watched his mother as she bent over her sewing. She looked thin and tired.

"Right now?" she asked. "Before the winter, Aaron?"

Aaron nodded. "Rosina can help you, Ma. She could stay home in Mary's place whenever you needed her, couldn't she, Ma?"

Mrs. Lyon shook her head and looked thoughtfully at her only son. Finally she said, "I'll think about it." And two days later she said, "The next time you go to Ashfield for goods, you might speak to Mrs. Elmer and see if she wants Mary for a few months."

Ashfield was a small town five miles south of Buckland Center. It had several stores, a judge's office, an inn, and a grammar school.

Before the week was out, Aaron returned from Ashfield with word that the Elmers would keep Mary for the winter.

"Would you like to go to school, Mary?" her mother asked at the supper table that evening.

Mary looked across the table, first at Aaron and then at her younger sisters. "Me?" Mary cried.

"Yes, you, Mary. Aaron says you should go."

"Oh, could I, Ma?" questioned Mary. Then her face fell and she said, "But what would you and Aaron do?"

Her mother half smiled and glanced up quickly at Aaron. "Oh, I guess we can manage. Besides, Rosina is old enough to help me. The Elmers will take you. What do you say?"

Mary threw Aaron a grateful look. "I can't think of anything I'd rather do. I do so want to go, Ma."

During the days that followed, excitement was high in the Lyon home. Mary was going to school again and live in town!

✳

On the morning of her departure, everyone was up early to help. Mrs. Lyon gave her a satchel to carry her clothes in, and Aaron took her shoes out to the barn to clean with a little bacon grease he had saved for that very purpose. Rushing up and down stairs to collect the few things Mary would want, Rosina and Freelove laughed gaily as if they were at a party. Yet if it weren't for the prospect of going to school, Mary would find it difficult to leave the family. She felt like laughing and crying all at the same time.

Soon Mary and Aaron were driving off in the wagon. They waved to Mother and the girls until they turned the bend in the road and the bright red and yellow maples hid the farmhouse from sight.

Mary wondered what it would be like living in the large two-story house on Main Street with the Elmers. "I'll probably have a hard time with the lessons," she thought. "It's so long since I have been to school." Deep inside, she was "scared," but she needn't have been.

Mr. and Mrs. John Elmer treated her as one of the family. The work was hard, but she had time to study. And she had a room upstairs to herself with a small table-desk that Mr. Elmer had made for his oldest child, a son who had accidentally drowned.

Mary worked carefully at her lessons and was at the head of the class in everything but grammar. That was hard for her. She was constantly mixing "were" and "was," and often had to return to the back bench to rewrite the "scribblyscrawl," as she called her poor penmanship.

Geography was different. "I like to make maps," she told Mr. Elmer, who looked curiously at the papers on her desk one evening.

"What do you call this one, Mary?" Mrs. Elmer asked.

"That's a map of the northern section of the country—but look at this one." Mary pulled a large, folded paper from the pile. It was a map she had made of the United States of America in color, with the Mississippi River and the section of the Louisiana Territory at the west.

Mary pointed to Massachusetts, outlined in red, and to the stretch of coastline from Salem to Plymouth. "Someday, who knows, I may travel as far away as Plymouth and the Atlantic Ocean. Do you suppose they still have Indians there?"

"Perhaps so," agreed Mr. Elmer. "Perhaps so. There are still some Indians in Deerfield—that was once the scene of bloody Indian wars, with the old Mohawks. But what do you know about Indians in Plymouth?"

"Well, it says in this book that King Philip attacked Swansea in the old Plymouth Colony. Listen to this." Mary read from Morse's *Geography:* " 'After slaughtering the cattle and plundering the houses, the Indians fired upon the inhabitants and killed and wounded several.' "

"Mary, are you going to be a teacher, like your sisters Electa and Jemima?" interrupted Mrs. Elmer.

"Maybe . . . I don't know though," said Mary. She hadn't intended to tell anyone, but she found herself explaining her plans to the Elmers. Their genuine kindness encouraged her.

"I think I've wanted to teach ever since I can remember anything at all. It's just that Mother needs me at home. Besides, I haven't been to school a full winter for years—not since Pa died."

Then the Elmers talked with her about the farm and Aaron and her mother, and for the first time since she had arrived

✻

at the Elmers', she was homesick. Often she had thought of home and had wished that she could tell the folks about the lessons, the maps, and the spelling bees, but never before had she felt lonesome for the mountain home.

Long after the Elmers had said good night and the children were in bed, Mary sat at her desk. It was raining heavily and the steady beat of the rain on the windows made her even more lonely. She rubbed her hand across the top of the table-desk, admiring, as she had so many times, the beautiful scroll patterning and the carved holder for the quill pens.

She thought about the grassy knolls near the woods, and the ferns and Indian pipes that grew there in profusion. The fruit trees would soon be in bloom, and there would be wild strawberries to pick. She could see the rivulet that wound its way among rocks and cliffs and gushed into the deep, craggy dells in springtime. Then, just beyond the borders of the farm, was the "top of the hill"—Putnam's Hill.

She slid into bed and tried to shut out the sound of the beating rain. It would soon be March and she would be ready to go home in time for the spring planting.

3

THE EMPTY FARMHOUSE

"Hello, everybody. I'm back," hallooed Mary as she scrambled down the side of the wagon. She took the satchel from Aaron's outstretched hand and bounded into the kitchen. Rosina and Freelove rushed at her happily and there were hugs all around.

"But where's Ma?" Mary asked. It wasn't like her mother not to be there at the kitchen door when she arrived from town. "Where is she?" Mary's voice was high and troubled.

"Sh-h-h," whispered Rosina, pointing to the closed door of the parlor. "Company."

"Company? But why didn't Aaron tell me? Who is it?"

"It's Mr. Taylor," said Freelove, putting her hands to her face and giggling. Rosina tried to hush Freelove.

"He's been helping with the garden," explained Rosina.

"With the garden? But I thought—" Mary always helped

with the spring planting. "I'm home in time," she thought. "Ma could have waited for me." She glanced at Rosina. She looked uneasy and disturbed.

"Ma," Mary called in defiance at the closed door. "I'm home!" Then, without waiting for an answer, she grabbed the satchel and ran upstairs. She wouldn't come down, she told herself, until "that man" had left the house. She pulled a box out from under the bed and packed away the schoolbooks, slate, and pens. She remembered Schoolmaster Higgins saying, "Too bad you're not a boy. I'd like to see what you would do if you could go to college."

"But I shan't go to school again, ever," she muttered. "Not and leave the family."

But she did, quite unexpectedly. She went the following summer and for the next two years off and on while she lived with the Woodwards. Mrs. Woodward, from below the Hollow, had come to ask for Mary's help on the farm. Although the Woodwards lived only three miles away, Mrs. Lyon decided to have Mary "live in" as Lovina had done.

"Do I have to stay, Ma?" Mary had asked. " I can walk home after the day's work is done. Then I could help you, too."

"Nonsense, Mary, there's no need," her mother replied rather sharply.

"But . . ."

"Mary, let's not talk about it any more. It's better that way. And besides, Mr. Woodward says there's a district school a few rods up the road, across from the Wares."

Mary was silent as they set the table for supper, but it wasn't the companionable silence they had known before the frequent visits from Mr. Taylor. This silence had something forced about it.

It was strange, the way her mother acted when Mr. Taylor came to the house. She brightened up and seemed less strained and tired. As the weeks went by, Mary noticed that her mother was more and more absent-minded. There was just no point either in arguing or asking questions. Her thoughts were apparently elsewhere. Mary would have to make her own decisions.

Each fall for the next two years, Mary worked at the Woodwards and lived in, canning, pickling, and doing the general housework. Then, every day after the noon meal when she was free, she would hurry off to the schoolhouse and study with the younger children.

"I'm doing better in grammar," she wrote Electa at the end of the second term. "I hope you'll think my penmanship has improved, too." She remembered how beautiful Electa had looked—tall and straight, with her father's dark eyes and black hair—that summer day when she married Ariel Moore. They had gone west to Ohio, and it took ten days to get a letter from her.

Mary returned from the Woodwards, this time to stay. It was the fall of 1809 and she was twelve years old. The winter passed busily and Mary helped her mother with all the chores. Then came the early March day that she grew up. The dishes were finished, and Mary sat doing some mending. The house was quiet.

"A penny for your thoughts," said Mrs. Lyon.

Mary hesitated. Her mother, she was certain, would not understand as completely as Electa, but she had no reason for not telling her.

✻

"I was just thinking about Mr. Porter, the schoolteacher. You know, he thinks I should go to an academy this winter."

"What did you tell him?"

"That I couldn't go. I told him you needed me on the farm."

Mrs. Lyon got up and poked the fire. Then she turned and sat down at the table opposite Mary. "There's something I've been meaning to tell you since you got home from the Woodwards. It's about me and the farm . . . and Mr. Taylor."

She talked quietly, explaining to Mary the plans already made: that she and Mr. Taylor were getting married in April, that Aaron would have the farm, and that the girls would go with her to the large Taylor house in Ashfield. Mary listened but said nothing. She couldn't believe it: her mother was going to get married again!

"I should have told you before."

Mary sat tight-lipped. Her mother continued to explain, "I gave the farm to Aaron. When I told him about Mr. Taylor, he said it was all right—he could manage. And your sisters will be able to finish school in Ashfield."

"Of course, I . . . I had to know," Mary said softly. She felt choked. She tried to go on with the mending, but she couldn't. She had to talk with Aaron and make him see that it wasn't all right at all.

"But it is, Mary," he said firmly. Mary watched him as he went about the milking, wondering how he could be so accepting.

"Why, Aaron, why?" she pressed for a reason.

"I told you, Mary. It will be easier for Ma. Mr. Taylor can give her a good home."

"And what's wrong with the farm?" she said defensively. "What would Pa say if—" She shook her head, blinking back the tears.

"But Pa has been gone eight years, Mary, and Ma has worked real hard."

"I've helped, Aaron, and I could help Ma more. No matter what Mr. Porter says, I don't need to go to school."

"It won't make any difference now—Ma's decided."

"Oh, Aaron," she cried. "I hate Mr. Taylor. How could he take her away—and the girls, too. I hate him!" She felt an ache in her throat. "The house will be so empty."

Crying softly, Mary buried her head in her hands.

"Don't cry," Aaron said. "It will be all right, really it will. You'll stay here at the farm with me and we'll make out."

But thirteen-year-old Mary cried. She cried for the father she missed and for the uncertainty of things to come. She was aware that Aaron had finished milking and had come to her side. He said nothing, just stood there watching, concerned.

At last, brushing back the tears, Mary said, "They'll wonder where we are." Then she picked up a pail of milk and followed Aaron into the house.

In the weeks that followed, there was no time in the bustling household to think about her own sorrow and feelings. There was a wedding to plan for and things to pack and put away. Together they sorted the blankets and quilts, those to go with her mother and those to stay at the farm for Mary and Aaron. They sewed and mended, and they packed the food in baskets and pails—Baldwin apples for pies, jars of preserved peaches and plums, and a jug of maple syrup.

By the time Mr. Taylor arrived with horse and buggy on the morning of April 20, 1810, the wedding day, the last box

＊

had been packed and the trunks closed. While Aaron helped Mr. Taylor put the boxes and bundles into the trunk of the buggy, Mary stayed in the kitchen. She washed the dishes and cleared the table. Then she tied back her hair with a brown ribbon that matched the belt of her gingham dress. She sat, ready for her mother's wedding, and waited until Aaron called her.

"Time to go, Mary," he called from the open door.

"Mary," her mother said, coming from the bedroom into the kitchen, her face sober and questioning. Mary looked up at her mother, lovely in her gray alpaca dress trimmed with white ruching at the throat and cuffs. "Mary," she repeated, "is there anything I can do before . . . before we go to the church?"

"No, Ma," Mary answered quickly. "Aaron and I will make out just fine." She'd manage somehow. There was nothing more her mother could leave or take away.

Mrs. Lyon looked long at her daughter and said, "You've been a good daughter to me always, Mary. Come, now. Your sisters are waiting for us."

"I'm coming, Ma," Mary said.

Then Mary climbed up onto the seat beside her two sisters. Her eyes blurred with tears, she was unaware of the countryside, unaware of the long pull for the horses up the steep hills, the occasional view of the valley below, and the winding path over the plank bridges. She only knew that she would be alone, that life on Putnam's Hill had changed.

At the wedding she sat near Grandmother Shepard and Uncle Isaac. She remembered suddenly the time her grandmother had told about the family, how the Shepards had objected to her mother's marriage to Aaron Lyon. He was, they complained, an ordinary farmer of little means and ten years older than their daughter, a frail girl of seventeen. And he hadn't been properly baptized. She wondered what Grandmother Shepard thought about this wedding.

"Dearly beloved . . ." Rev. Amos Smith read the service for his niece. The Smiths had been early settlers in Ashfield and had held the first public worship in their own home. Both sons had become ministers, and Amos succeeded his father Chileab Smith as pastor of the Baptist Church at Four Corners.

"You know where Chileab's Hill is, Mary, about a mile north of South Hadley? Well, that was named for your great-grandfather," Grandmother Shepard liked to boast. "Wish you might have known him. He wasn't ordained until he was eighty years old, but he lived to be ninety-five."

"I wish I might have known him," Mary thought, "and I wish my own father had lived. . . ."

When the service was over, Mary stood quietly beside Aaron as the congregation sang "Blest Be the Tie That Binds." She wanted to sing, but the words wouldn't come. It was like a deep ache inside.

A few minutes later she watched her mother climb happily and proudly into the buggy. It was all over. She turned to Aaron and said, "I'm going home."

"We'll take you as far as the Hollow," called Mrs. Woodward, hurrying away from the cluster of friends that had waited to see the Taylors leave. So Aaron and Mary rode back, Mary steeling herself against Mrs. Woodward's constant chatter.

"She meant well," Aaron said as they climbed Putnam's Hill toward home.

※

Mary nodded her understanding, brushing back the tears.

"She's too young," Mrs. Woodward had said to her husband later.

"But she's a big girl and a fine worker. She's as capable as her mother any day," he answered brusquely.

"I know, I know," agreed Mrs. Woodward. "Still, I'm sorry for her—only thirteen."

It was midafternoon when Mary and Aaron returned to the empty farmhouse. "You call me if you need me," Aaron had said as he went about the usual chores.

Mary wandered through the house, first into the parlor and then the downstairs bedroom. A few ribbons were on the dresser, and an old pair of knit gloves. She pulled open the top drawer and tossed them into it. Then hurriedly she picked up the coverlet that had been left for her on the bedside chair. It was the blue and white blanket that she and her mother had quilted last fall. She took it upstairs to her own room and packed it in the chest.

Slowly and deliberately, she changed from the brown cambric into the homespun flannel dress, took the brown ribbon off her hair, and, picking up Webster's *The Speller*, sat down in the window seat and began to read aloud.

In a little while she thought of Aaron, working alone outdoors, hurt perhaps, and afraid to say anything that would trouble her. She put on her heavy shoes and went downstairs into the cheerless kitchen.

She filled her arms with wood from the woodbox and started the fire. Then, gathering up the dishes on the shelf, she set the table. "I think," she said to herself, "I'll heat up the stew for Aaron and bake some of those apple dumplings he likes."

The butter churn had been placed in the corner. She brought it out to have it ready for the morning. And then she noticed that Freelove had left a doll on the bench near the loom. She put it in the parlor. "I guess your Ma has gone too," she sighed.

She hurried through the kitchen and out into the barn to call Aaron for supper. She found him mixing the feed for the sheep. She leaned against the stall, waiting for him to finish, watching him.

"Supper's ready," she announced.

"Are you all right, Mary?" he wanted to know.

She hesitated for just a moment and then looked at his strained face. "Yes, Aaron, and don't poke," she said in a matter-of-fact manner. "Supper's all hot."

"After supper," she thought, "I'll bring down my collection of weeds from the loft—and my books—and maybe I'll move my things into Ma's room off the kitchen."

It wasn't easy for Mary at first. At times she resented the kindness of friends, who sympathized with her and moralized at her. But she managed the house well and she had time to roam the hills and add to her specimens. She borrowed books from Mr. Porter, the schoolmaster, and read the lessons to Aaron whenever she could get him to listen.

One warm June day she went out to work in the garden and found Mr. Porter in the yard talking to Aaron. Their voices were low and they looked serious.

"Hello, Mr. Porter," she called. "What brings you to our mountain home this warm day?"

"To tell the truth, I came to talk about you," he said.

Mary smiled at the "deacon," for people around Buckland always called him that. He was a pleasant, gentle man and

✼

given to indulging in light humor. Mary laughed and stopped the weeding to talk with him.

"I was just telling Aaron here that I thought it was about time you went back to school."

Mary looked puzzled. "But I'm staying home with Aaron on the farm, Deacon. Besides, Mother says that I have had more schooling than most girls my age."

Mary recalled how the neighbors had complained to her mother about her studying grammar and penmanship at the district school last fall.

"The neighbors said," she continued, "that girls like me should be satisfied with reading, spelling, and needlework. I'm not much at needlework, but I can bake and weave. Once last winter, when Mother was sick, I went over to Conway in her place and wove a blanket for Mrs. Field."

"That's right, she did," agreed Aaron proudly, "and we bought shoes for all the family with the money she earned."

"But I think you should go to school, Mary—and to an academy, soon, and Aaron says he'll gladly pay you a dollar a week, just as he would a regular housekeeper."

"Aaron shouldn't pay me . . ." protested Mary.

"I want to, Mary," interrupted Aaron. "That way you can save some money for school."

"I can get you a teaching position in Shelburne Falls as soon as you have had a few more terms at the district school. You save enough from your teaching, and you'd be ready for an academy after that. Think about it, Mary," said Mr. Porter.

She *had* thought about teaching, but she'd never really thought about going to an academy. That was where well-to-do girls of the best families went, not farm girls.

"What do you think, Aaron?" she asked cautiously.

He answered without hesitation, "It's up to you, Mary." She knew by his smile and by his answer that he was pleased. It was as though a welcoming door had opened. She felt less lonely.

"I'll come down in the fall after the harvest," said Mary, smiling back at her brother.

4
GROWING UP

Mary was fifteen years old when the War of 1812 broke out. Neighbors called it Mr. Madison's War, and very few of the boys she knew went away to fight in it. She couldn't quite understand why Uncle Nate felt he had to join the volunteers of New York State, but she did think he looked splendid as he marched away.

She was glad that Aaron's name wasn't listed among the men ordered to Boston to defend the coast. He had finally gotten up courage to ask Armilla Alden, oldest daughter of Rev. John and Nancy Alden, to marry him. They had postponed the wedding date twice because of the war. Now they would be married in early May.

"You can stay with us, Mary," Aaron had said cheerfully. "This will always be your home, but you won't need to do the housework when we're married. And you'll be able to go to school as you planned."

GROWING UP

During the time she had kept house for Aaron, she had studied at the district school whenever she could be spared. At the mountain home she made and sold butter, pickles, and canned fruit. And she spent long hours at the loom, weaving mats and woolen cloth that she sold to neighbors and friends.

When she had earned five dollars or more from her handwork and from housekeeping, she went to Ashfield and banked her earnings with Mr. White.

"Mr. White will take care of your savings," Aaron told her. "Mother left the legacy with him, you know." Mr. White was a judge and lived on Main Street in Ashfield.

It was February 28, Mary's fifteenth birthday. She dressed slowly and carefully, putting on the new linsey-woolsey dress, the first she had made since her mother left the farmhouse. She had made it all, from the spinning of the wool to the sewing. Pleased with the results, she looked at herself for a long time in the small mirror over the dresser. She wondered if Aaron would notice. He probably wouldn't or, if he did, he wouldn't say a word. No matter, she was happy.

She spent longer than usual brushing and braiding the red curls. Then she pinned the braids into a roll and again looked into the mirror. "I look all of twenty," she thought.

At breakfast she announced, "There's a school in Shelburne Falls I can have." Two of her sisters had taught in the Falls, a town about nine miles north of Buckland on the Deerfield River.

"Are you going to take it?" Aaron asked eagerly.

Mary shook her head. "No, not now," she said emphatically. "There's a new school for girls in Greenfield. I'm going to see Mr. White and find out how much money I have—

✳

maybe there's enough." Greenfield meant an even longer trip for Mary. It was some twenty miles east.

Aaron watched Mary move briskly about the room, putting the dishes away and clearing the table. "And I'll help you all I can," he assured her.

"Don't wait supper for me," she told Aaron later as she rode off on Old Tom. "I'll try to get back before dark."

Mary liked to visit Mr. White. She would sit in the large Windsor chair in his study, where as Justice of the Peace he tried his cases, and listen with rapt attention while he told of his studies at Yale. Sometimes she talked to him at length, telling him about her schoolwork, about the books she had borrowed from his library, or about her own thoughts. In the spring she brought him the first of the Mayflowers from the woods, and in the winter, pine cones for the fireplace.

Today she had but one question to ask: "Do I have enough money to go to school in Greenfield?" And she proudly placed a small bag of money on his desk.

Mr. White pushed back his glasses and looked at Mary in surprise. He motioned to her to sit down. "I'm confused, Mary," he said. "I figured you were planning to teach school this fall in Shelburne."

"No," she said with quiet conviction. "I've changed my mind. There's a new girls' school in Greenfield I would like to go to."

Glancing at her quickly, he picked up the bag and emptied it. "I thought you wanted to teach," he said.

"Yes, someday," she replied earnestly.

"But not this year? Is that it?"

She nodded. "That's right. Mr. Porter says he has taught **me** all he can at the district school, but I don't yet feel I know all I should to teach. Couldn't I . . . don't I have money enough to go to grammar school first?"

In spite of herself, her voice faltered. His kind face looked anxious. It troubled her. Was he cross at her?

"What about Aaron and the farm?" he asked.

"Aaron is getting married in May, and he says they can get along without me if I care to go."

His sober expression softened a bit. Then he took a large ledger off the shelf, opened it, and read: " 'Mary M. Lyon, total savings to date, exclusive of the legacy, $24.75.' " He frowned and shook his head.

"With the six dollars you brought today, you could pay for half a term, not counting board and room. Then there's the coach fare. I'd say if you can earn that much again . . ."

Mary wasn't listening. She didn't hear the rest of the sentence. "Not this year?" she said anxiously.

"No, Mary, unless . . ."

"Unless what?" Mary's eyes brightened for a moment.

"Unless you want to touch the legacy."

Quick tears started to Mary's eyes. "I couldn't, Mr. White. Father meant it for me when I was twenty-one."

She wished she hadn't come. Nothing mattered now, nothing—her new blue dress, her fifteenth birthday. . . . There was no point in riding over to see her mother and sisters. Besides, her mother wouldn't understand. Who cared whether she went to grammar school?

After buying a few things at Parker's store, she rode slowly back along the trail, arriving home well before sundown.

"It's no use," she explained to Aaron at supper. "I haven't enough money. I might just as well forget about it." She tried to keep her voice steady. "It's no use, Aaron."

※

"You can do it another year, Mary," he ventured, looking at her thoughtfully.

"Another year, another year," she said unhappily. "I don't want to wait another year. I'm fifteen already."

"What did Mr. White say?"

"Just what you said—wait another year."

"I'll sell some of the sheep," he offered, thinking that Mary was far too bright to stay home much longer. "They should bring a good price this season."

"Oh, no, Aaron," she said firmly. "You need the sheep. You're getting married soon. I'll study with Mr. Porter a little longer."

Aaron looked troubled. Why was grammar school so expensive? He didn't know why a girl wanted an education, but then, Mary did, and she should have the opportunity as well as any boy. "Couldn't we ask Mother and Mr. Taylor for money? I think they'd . . ."

"No, Aaron," interrupted Mary, pressing her lips together tightly. "I'll earn the money myself," she added confidently. "I guess fifteen isn't so old after all."

Back in the closet went the birthday dress and the straw bonnet. She had work to do if the house was to be ready for Armilla Alden's arrival. She decided to move her things back to the upstairs bedroom she had once shared with Rosina.

On the oak floor she laid the hooked rugs she had worked on through many a winter's evening. At the windows that looked out onto the pasture she hung red cambric curtains, and on the west wall the sampler that Grandmother Lyon had made as a young woman.

When May came, it would be time enough to talk to Mr.

Porter about a teaching job. Meanwhile she would work and save for the academy. Maybe someday she could go.

On the flyleaf of the book *Geography Made Easy,* she wrote: "It is always necessary to distinguish between the very difficult and the impossible."

5

SOME BEGINNINGS

Two years later, in the spring of 1814, Mary went to teach at Shelburne Falls. Though she spent some Sundays and vacations at the farmhouse, she earned her board by living and working at the homes of pupils.

"You would earn more if you stayed home," Armilla said one day. "This way, you make only seventy-five cents a week plus board."

Mary stood in the kitchen door, watching her sister-in-law churn the butter with a steady beat of the paddle. Armilla was a pretty, mild woman, content with the endless household tasks and the care of her young son, Aaron Ezra, born the summer before.

It was hard to explain to Armilla just how she felt about teaching. Armilla had finished at the academy in Amherst but had been glad to put away the books. "I'd rather have a husband than a job," she said simply.

SOME BEGINNINGS

Mary smiled. "But that's actually twenty-five cents more than Electa made a week. You're right though, Armilla—I could earn more selling canned goods and woolen blankets."

And there were times when she thought she should. "If I ever get through this term without being dismissed, I shall never teach again," she confessed to Aaron one evening. "I guess I'm not the good teacher Electa was. I laugh when I should be serious, and then I'm in for trouble."

But Mary wasn't really discouraged. In a letter to Electa she wrote, that very evening, "I'm more determined than ever to become a good teacher."

To Aaron she said, "Maybe I don't have enough work for the children. It isn't easy to keep them busy all the time, with forty in the room. And two of the girls, the older Miller girls, finish before the others have hardly started."

Maybe, too, she should separate the pupils and put the older boys on the front benches. Perhaps that would stop the giggling. It was mostly Amos Fiske, though. He was a show-off.

It seemed as though he just had to cause trouble and get attention. If he wasn't waving his hand in the air to ask permission to get a drink or leave the room, he would put his foot out to trip anyone who passed near him.

One day the room was unusually restless and noisy. Mary looked down from the high desk and closed the book from which she had been reading to the class. Glancing quickly at the boys, she noticed a telltale piece of string hanging out of Amos' pocket. He had brought a forbidden slingshot into the schoolroom.

"What is it now, Amos? What do you have?" she asked crossly. She pushed aside the papers on her desk and climbed

※

down from the stool. Amos, a big, awkward boy, sat unmoved.

"Bring whatever you have and come here, Amos," she demanded.

But Amos sat. Mary took a deep breath and, repeating her command in a low but firm voice, stood quietly waiting.

"I hate to lick you, Amos, but if you force me to . . ."

"I tell you," Amos said curtly, "I didn't do a thing, Miss Lyon."

The battle line was drawn. She had no choice but to make it clear to the pupils that she was the "boss." Her face flushed and angry, she reached for the whip hanging on the wall.

"I hope I never have to whip a boy again," Mary told Jemima afterward. Though her sister no longer taught school, Mary found her a patient and helpful listener.

"I ought to be able to make them behave without whipping them," she said seriously.

"Did you ever try sending them out into the hallway?" Jemima asked.

"Yes, but that didn't work either. Amos and John took all the pegs off the wall and piled the clothes hit-and-miss in a corner." It suddenly seemed funny to Mary, and they both laughed at the prank.

"Don't sit down, even for a moment," Jemima advised. "I seldom use the desk or the high stool. It helps keep order to be on your feet." She paused and smiled. "The children never know where you'll turn up next in the room."

It was the constant whispering that concerned Mary most. "Give them time to play outdoors," Jemima suggested. "Get them tired and they'll run off some of that excess energy."

It worked; even Amos was quieter. Mary not only organized indoor games, but went outdoors and played with the children. Often, while the bigger boys and girls played more boisterous games—Needle's Eye or Kitty's Corner—she joined the younger children in Here We Stand Around the Ring.

And she assigned to different pupils each week the daily tasks of bringing in the firewood, stoking the stove, cleaning the room, sweeping the floor, and filling the water pail. Routine and busy hands made the days go better. She couldn't be sure she taught any better, but there was less noise and almost no whispering.

She needn't worry this spring about visiting day, when Mr. Porter and members of the school committee came to test the pupils. She would always remember that first spring visit. She had just reprimanded Amos for pulling Lovinda's braids when she saw Mr. Evans, chairman of the committee, standing in the open doorway.

"They didn't know a thing," she confessed later to Jemima. Even as she told her sister of the many mistakes the pupils had made, she felt nervous and chilled. "Why, Lucy Miller answered that three-fourths of thirteen was eight! I couldn't believe it," Mary explained.

"What did Mr. Evans say?" Jemima asked.

"Nothing, that was the bad part of it. He heard them read and recite, but left without saying a thing," Mary sighed. "But he didn't look too pleased."

"And Mr. Porter?"

Mary smiled. "He never complained. He only said on leaving that he hoped the children would improve a bit the next year, especially in arithmetic."

"I ought to study again," she thought. "I ought to go to grammar school or an academy."

✳

Girls like Mary who had been brought up on a farm usually married in their teens. If not, their family began to worry about having an "old maid" aunt on their hands. If they did go beyond the district school, it was expected that they were preparing for missionary work.

But not Mary. She had never thought about the missionary field. In fact, she couldn't be sure she was a good Christian. She went to church on Sunday, but she had grave doubts about her belief. The minister often urged her to join the church, and sometimes she felt she would, if only she didn't have to be baptized in Clesson's River.

But she would go to school, and she would study for a full term again.

"I'll really go next year," she told Mr. White on one of her visits to Ashfield. She smiled confidently and said, "By that time I should have enough money to stay for a full term."

"That's right, Mary," he agreed. "And I have good news for you. Mr. Sanderson is opening an academy right here in Ashfield."

Sanderson Academy opened in April of 1817, and Mary was one of the first to arrive. She made arrangements to live with Mrs. Nellie Bascomb on South Street and to earn her room and board by helping with the housework.

Each night Mary worked late at her studies, not snuffing out the candles until almost midnight. She shut herself up with the science books that Mr. Burritt lent her and amazed him with her progress.

"I'd like to see what she could have done in college," Mr. Burritt told the headmaster, Mr. Sanderson. "If only she hadn't been a girl. . . ."

"No one studies like Miss Lyon," said Amanda White,

SOME BEGINNINGS

Mr. White's oldest daughter, an attractive, slender girl of nineteen. She and her younger sister, Hannah, went to many of the same classes as Mary, for Mr. White highly approved of education for girls. His wife often complained, however. "They'll injure their health, studying too much," she told him. "It's unladylike. I surely could teach my girls all they need to know."

Sewing, knitting, embroidery, and mending were all the accomplishments most of the Ashfield girls were taught. "I would rather they learned more than that. They'll make better wives," Mr. White would say with a kind of finality in his voice.

"Don't you ever sleep, Mary?" Amanda asked one day after the dismissal bell had rung.

Mary looked up from the paper she was writing and smiled at her friend. "Why, of course I do. Why do you ask me?"

"Oh, Father says you study all the time and that I should follow your example," said Amanda, putting on her thick wool coat, eager to leave for home. "I think you're the smartest girl I ever knew. By the way, Mr. Burritt and Mr. Sanderson were talking about your work the other day."

Mary's cheeks flushed. "You shouldn't listen, Amanda."

"Don't you want to know what they said?" Amanda teased. "They were talking about a celestial map of yours." Mr. Elijah Burritt had recently graduated from Williams College, and he was an exciting teacher. Mary found the study of astronomy with him a "real delight."

"Amanda!" Mary scolded. "Stop it, Amanda. I won't listen to you."

"All right, but I'm going home." Amanda put on the

crocheted head scarf, showing off a fashionable fringe of curls on her forehead. "How do you like my hair?" she asked.

"It's very becoming," said Mary impatiently.

"You weren't even looking, Mary. You certainly can be provoking. When are you going to put your hair up?"

Mary shook her head. "When I have time, Amanda. It's much easier to handle in braids. I find it doesn't always stay up well."

"Let me fix it for you sometime," insisted Amanda.

"Sometime, maybe," said Mary indifferently. She couldn't be bothered with combs and hairpins. She felt somewhat irritated by Amanda's concern.

"Don't bother me now about my hair. I've got work to do on the almanac that Mr. Burritt assigned for astronomy."

Mary spent the rest of the afternoon in the science room, working on the almanac and reading the atlas that came in the pocket of Dwight's *Geography Text*. It fascinated her to compute travel time to London and European cities she had never known. She hurried through the lessons in arithmetic and Latin to study science. There didn't seem to be enough hours in a day to do all she wanted.

One morning after class Mr. Burritt congratulated Mary on her Latin. "I hear," he said earnestly, "that you outdid yourself in class today. If you keep this up, we won't have lessons for next term, Miss Lyon."

"It was nothing, Mr. Burritt. Dr. Sanderson gave me a copy of Adams' *Latin Grammar* Friday afternoon. 'To keep me busy,' he said. So I took it home and studied it all week end, including Sunday."

Mr. Burritt looked up from his desk and asked, "Is it

true that you recited the entire book, lesson by lesson, and answered every question about the grammar?"

"Yes, the entire book. I just got started and couldn't leave it alone."

She waited for him to reprove her for studying on Sunday, but he didn't. Instead he chuckled and went away laughing at the story. But she didn't find it at all funny, and she wondered if everyone in school had heard about it.

6

A LOCKET FOR LOVE

It was a fine day that memorable Monday—green and gold, with great clusters of dandelions in bloom on the sloping lawn, and the air still and warm. Mary was sitting on the porch at Mrs. Bascomb's working out an arithmetic assignment when she first saw him. He was wearing a brown-striped broadcloth suit, with matching kid gloves and soft hat. She noticed his brisk walk and looked up to watch him as he came down the street.

When he reached the gate, he put down his heavy bag and, leaning on the fence, smiled a slow, bright smile. She glanced up at him uneasily.

"You must be the new teacher from the city?" Her statement became a question. He bowed briefly.

"Yes, my name is Ferry, William Ferry, and I'd be pleased if you would direct me to the academy."

"I'd be happy to. I'm Mary Lyon." And without a thought

A LOCKET FOR LOVE

of what the neighbors might think or say, she was walking down Main Street and talking freely with this tall, handsome young man.

In the days that followed, Mary hurried through her lessons to spend more of her time on the compositions for English classes. She found herself longing for Mr. Ferry's approval.

"I no longer find English grammar so difficult," she wrote Electa. "Even my work in arithmetic improves. I may yet be able to teach long division successfully."

One Saturday morning in June, Mrs. Bascomb called to her from the bottom of the hall stairs. "Company, Miss Lyon—for you." Brushing back her hair and putting on a shawl, she thought with pleasure, "Perhaps the Whites are driving to Greenfield."

But as she entered the hallway, she saw Mr. Ferry standing near the front window. As she crossed the parlor, he turned and walked toward her. Mary felt her face flush.

"Why, it's you, Mr. Ferry," she said in a low voice. "Mrs. Bascomb didn't tell me . . ."

"I came to call, Miss Lyon. I wanted to ask you to drive over with me to Buckland tomorrow afternoon. Mr. Sanderson told me you had once lived there and I thought you might show me the country—you know it so well." He looked questioningly at her, then his face was softened by a smile.

Mary was not used to young gentlemen callers. But she was strangely moved by Mr. Ferry's charm.

"I hope you will be free to come," he added.

"Yes, thank you, Mr. Ferry. Yes, I'd be pleased to drive out with you," she murmured.

The next evening, as Mary brushed her hair, she looked

into the mirror at her flushed face. It seemed as though she had known William Ferry all her life.

He had talked so easily about himself, and his genuine interest drew her out. He spoke about his family in Oswego, New York, and told her about his illness with rheumatic fever when he was fifteen, and that, too frail to carry out the work of the farm with his father, he had worked in a store for three years and saved money for a college education.

Mary was touched by the picture of the lonely boy who had worked his way through college and later studied theology with Dr. Gardiner Spring, minister of the Brick Presbyterian Church in New York City.

Suddenly he had leaned toward her. "And you, Miss Lyon? Mr. Burritt has told me a great deal about you. He says you wish to go to college."

"Yes," she said wistfully. "I've wanted to do that for many years."

"And so you shall, I am sure."

After that, William found many opportunities to be with Mary. Sometimes they went for a drive in a carriage he hired, but more often they walked to Ashfield Pond or to Hawley, five miles away, where her sister Jemima lived.

One sunny afternoon they went as far as the Baptist Church in East Buckland, where Mary's mother had been married eight years before. They sat for a while on the steps of the small wooden building across from the burial ground.

"What was your father like?" William asked.

"Like my brother Aaron, I guess. That's what my mother always said. He never talked much, but was kind and gentle, with eyes as blue as the gentian. All I remember clearly is sitting in his lap and reading to him. I was five when he died."

They were silent for a while. The hurt in Mary's eyes kept him from further questions about her childhood. Instead he asked, "Is your brother married?"

"Oh, yes." Mary brightened as she told of the family and the children—Nancy, now three, and Ezra, just a year old. "Aaron and Armilla live in the old mountain home on Putnam's Hill. I call their home mine. That's the only family I have—my mother left to marry again when I was thirteen."

"I'm sorry, Mary. I didn't know." William explained.

She shook her head. "That's all right, William. It doesn't trouble me any more."

Suddenly she sprang up and started down the steps. At the bottom step, she turned and asked quietly, "Shall we stop in to see the Whites on our return?"

"Would you like to, Mary?"

"Yes, and I rather think they will be expecting you from what Amanda said—something about a church meeting."

William nodded and frowned slightly. "Mrs. White has insisted on my meeting with the Circle on Foreign Missions. But tell me, when are we going to see your family on Putnam's Hill?"

Mary felt her pulse quicken. She looked up at William, her face alight. "Do you want to meet my family, William?"

"I want to very much, Mary. And you?"

"Yes," she whispered. "Yes, I'd like that. And I'd like to take you to the top of Putnam's Hill."

It was several weeks before Mary and William called on her family. It seemed to Mary that there had never been

※

such a beautiful day as the one she and William chose to walk to the hill. The blue sky was all but cloudless, and the view from her special rock at the top of the hill extended for miles on every side.

As they climbed the hill together, Mary told him about her sisters, how they had left home to teach school and then had married and gone away. She told him how Aaron had looked after her and how she had kept house for him until he, too, got married.

"I used to come to this spot on the hill whenever anything special or different happened in my life," she said. "I came here the day my mother told me she was getting married . . . and the day I found I could go to school again, and . . ."

She thought of the many times she had come to look off into the valley, to see Clesson's River and the white spire of the church in Buckland Center, to feel renewed and more content. And now there was William to see it and to share it.

"Do you like the view, William?"

"Yes, it's magnificent," he answered quickly.

Then, taking Mary's hand, he placed in it a small gold locket. "A gift, Mary, for this special day of ours. It was my mother's."

It was a round locket framed in tiny pearls. Mary thought it lovelier than any piece of jewelry she had ever seen.

"Wear it for me," he said as he fastened it around her throat. Then he drew her close. Slowly they followed the winding path down to the mountain home.

Mary had gone to Mr. Burritt's science room and laboratory to repeat an experiment he had performed. Intent on

A LOCKET FOR LOVE

examining bacteria through a microscope, she hadn't heard William enter the room. As she picked up the glass slide and placed it on a tray, she suddenly saw him standing beside the table.

Flushing slightly, she said, "How long have you been standing there?"

"Just long enough to wonder what you are up to."

She tried to tell him about the experiment and offered to let him look through the microscope, but he wasn't listening. She could tell. His face was stern and unsmiling. "I have something to show you as soon as you're finished."

Mary pushed aside the pitcher and slides, took off the cambric apron and hung it on a nail back of the door. Then she carefully placed the microscope in the case. Microscopes were rare in small schools, and the students had been given special directions on the care of this one.

Walking around the table, Mary started to sit down on a high stool near him. "Not here," he said. "I'd rather go where we'll be alone."

He said very little as they walked the Buckland Road along Ashfield Pond. Finally he handed her a letter postmarked New York City.

She read:

April the 12th, 1818

Dear Mr. Ferry:
　　Yours received. The Missionary Society wishes to offer you a post on Mackinac Island, Michigan, and it is our sincere hope that you will be able to serve. Chippewa Indians there need Christian conversion. . . .

There was more to the letter but she couldn't read on. She felt heartsick.

*

"It's what you want?" she faltered.

"Yes, just what I have wanted, Mary. After a year in Michigan, I can be a minister either there or somewhere in New England—if you'd think better of it."

William put the letter back in his coat pocket. A sigh escaped him. "If only I didn't have to leave you, Mary. Will you wait for me?"

She nodded her head. Wait for him? What else was there to do or say? She got up quickly and pulled her coat around her. "Let's go back, William," she urged.

"But your answer, Mary. Do you think I should go?"

"Of course, William. You'll be a fine minister, and I'll be right here, waiting."

Michigan was miles away from Massachusetts, and there would be unknown dangers in Indian country. She looked at his strikingly handsome face and felt the rush of disappointment and fear. He would be gone soon, and only now did she sense her need and her real love for him.

She added to herself, "All my life I'd wait for you." She wanted to cry, "Take me with you."

"Write to me! You will? Soon?"

The morning of departure soon came. The coachman flicked the whip and the coach was on its way to Buffalo. He was gone. A year to wait. It was like a dull ache to think of it.

A few days later she went to see Mr. White. She had decided. She, too, would leave Ashfield. That was it. She couldn't and she wouldn't stay on for the summer at Sanderson without William, reminded of him constantly.

"I want to use some of my legacy, Mr. White," she said,

hurrying on to explain that she wanted to study at Amherst Academy.

Mr. Burritt had often urged Mary to go to Amherst and study chemistry and physics there with Professor Graves.

In answer to Mary's request, Mr. White had the money for her within the week. "What are your plans after the summer is over?"

"I have none at present."

"Well, think about coming back to Sanderson. If you do, let me know. I am sure I can arrange some help."

Mr. White's kindness moved Mary deeply. She was grateful that he hadn't asked her why she was going, even if he could imagine why. With his help she had found at least a temporary solution for life without William. She would try to forget her loneliness.

Amherst was a day's journey south across the Connecticut River. There she would study and work hard. When William returned from the West she could plan for a new life.

7

A NEW HOME

Looking back on it afterward, Mary believed that the year 1818 had flown by. But that was because she had forgotten how long were the months before the first letter came from William. Meanwhile she finished the three-week session at Amherst Academy. In July she went to the mountain home with Aaron and the family, helping Armilla with the housework and looking after the two little girls, Nancy and baby Lucy. Ezra, a sturdy lad of five, spent most of his time trailing his father around the farm and feeding the animals.

It was late August when a letter postmarked Michigan was delivered at the Lyon household. Armilla shouted the news from the kitchen door. But Mary took the letter upstairs to read it first alone. Carefully she broke the seal.

At first glance she was disappointed. It was just a record of events. As she read on, she realized that William meant to share the story of his journey and to tell it for her brother Aaron and his wife.

What he had said to her alone she would find in the closing lines. "I can't tell you how much I miss you. It's as though my new life here were half a life without you."

Then she reread the letter, fascinated: Buffalo and the trip on the steamboat *Walk-on-the-Water* up Lake Erie, long delays in Detroit, a schooner for the last leg of the trip to Mackinac Island. He had found a boarding place with a Mrs. Dousman and her family, who lived in one of the few houses in a settlement of wigwams.

That letter was the high point of the summer. Before summer ended Mary had moved back to Mrs. Bascomb's to begin the senior course at the academy, this time with enough linen and quilts in her trunk to pay for room and board. Mrs. Bascomb had accepted the offer of her handwork, and with this arrangement, Mary was free to give all her attention to her studies.

"But Mary," Armilla had objected, "when I think of what you're giving away, your blankets and all, I wonder if you really should."

Mary gave Armilla a hug. "Don't you fret. I can always come home and weave. Right now I want to go back to Sanderson Academy, and I've decided that's the best way to do it."

Armilla, busy rolling out the dough, dropped the paddle. "I told Aaron I was sure you had plans of your own we knew nothing about. . . . Has he told you about our plans to go west, to Stockton, New York?"

"Plans to go west? Why, no, Armilla." She sat down op-

✱

posite Armilla at the kitchen table, no longer smiling.

"Aaron wants to take up land in New York State," Armilla said bluntly.

Go west? Aaron, go west? Why, he seldom left the farm to go to Uncle Nate's in Buckland Center, and only rarely went to Shelburne Falls with his family. This must be Armilla's decision.

As though she read her very thoughts, Armilla sat up stiffly, saying, "It's his decision, Mary. He's talked of nothing else since last summer."

"Then I'll talk to Aaron."

"I wish you would, Mary. I don't know how I can do it, with the baby coming in a few months and all that's to be done here. I told him you ought to know before you left for Ashfield." There was a note of desperation in Armilla's voice. Now it was Mary's turn to console her sister-in-law.

Aaron had meant to tell Mary when she first returned from Amherst but she had seemed worried and unhappy. Now he wished he had, for it might be difficult to convince her.

"You'll have to tell her soon, Aaron, or I shall," Armilla had said. And so she had.

Later, Aaron read to Mary some of the letters from Uncle Isaac, who had gone west the year before and settled in Stockton, New York. The letters were full of the advantages of living in the western country, with its great rivers and lakes and fertile soil.

Aaron paused and looked at Mary, but she said nothing.

"He says land can be purchased at a dollar and a quarter an acre—good land," Aaron continued. "Not this rocky hillside that we have struggled with all these years."

A NEW HOME

At last she said slowly, "Then I shouldn't go off to Sanderson and leave Armilla."

"Yes, you should, Mary. We'll not go anyway until spring." He hesitated, studying her sober face. "Perhaps you would go with us. You could teach out there. Uncle Isaac writes that they need schoolteachers badly."

"I couldn't, Aaron. Not now. But what will you do with the farm?"

"I've put it up for sale, and I'll sell it lock, stock, and barrel. We'll take only what we can carry in the wagon, and we'll stay with the Shepards until we build."

So it was all settled. It was too late for Aaron to change his plans, too late for her. Besides, William would expect to find her in Ashfield. But what would she do without her family and the little girls she had grown to love?

With gentle concern, Aaron was looking at her. "If I had any idea you were so . . . I wish that you . . ."

He broke off, paced a step or two, and turned back to the table. "You do want to stay in Ashfield, Mary?"

"Yes, Aaron."

But Mary spoke absently. Her heart had grown suddenly heavy. Everyone was going west. Yet in spite of her disappointment she couldn't be the one to make their leaving unpleasant.

"I'll be home in the spring to help you pack. . . . It's strange," she added, "I always thought I'd be the one to leave you."

"I know," he said. They sat silent for a while, watching Ezra as he piled wooden blocks into a small basket.

In March, Mary returned from Ashfield to the mountain home in time for the sugaring. The gray-barked maple trees

✺

in the upper pasture usually supplied enough syrup for the winter months. Aaron tapped the trees by driving in basswood spouts and collecting the sap in pails. Mary carried the pails to the tubs for boiling.

"When we are settled out there," Aaron said, "you can come and live with us."

"That's what Armilla keeps saying. You're good to me, Aaron, and I do hope you'll find it a right place to bring up the children."

Mary tried to keep the pain out of her voice. At times she felt selfish in not giving up her own plans and going with them, but they made no further attempt to urge her to go. Armilla would be busy with the new baby, Franklin Smith, born February 27, 1819, just one day before Mary's own birthday.

"I'm well," Armilla explained. "And Franklin is such an easy, happy baby, not like Lucy. And Ezra is a big boy."

Through the days that followed, Mary helped with the preparations for departure. She baked bread and pies, and cooked most of the food, enough to last them on the trip.

All the commotion brought back sharp memories of her mother's leaving, and she thought sadly of the miles that would separate them. But with determined self-control she sorted and packed their few possessions.

With the same self-control she bade them farewell the morning of May 10. The pressure of arms around her tore at her heart. Was it good-bye forever? Only baby Lucy cried. She hung on to Mary's skirts until her aunt was forced to pick her up and hold her for a while. Armilla scolded her, but she was still crying when the wagon disappeared from sight.

A NEW HOME

Mary walked slowly back into the house. The farmhouse that had been part of her life for twenty-two years was empty.

Mary was not to know a home again for another two years. She went from family to family, teaching school in Buckland and in Ashfield. Occasionally she spent a vacation at Uncle Nate's, and once in a while she stayed with Jemima, but she didn't return to Sanderson Academy for the senior course until the winter of 1821.

One afternoon in early fall, Mr. White called her into his office. "Mr. Burritt needs an assistant in his science classes. How about it, Mary?"

She hesitated; he continued, "And I would like to have you stay with us. What do you say?"

She was doubtful. How could she live with the Whites in that beautiful house? They were an "aristocratic family," as everyone knew, and bought their clothes in the city. Amanda had often told her of their trips to Boston, and how Morris, her oldest brother, had gone to Dartmouth College in New Hampshire in his own horse-drawn carriage, a gift of his father.

"It will mean you can finish the course and get your diploma," Mr. White explained.

"And Mrs. White?" Mary needed to know. Amanda and Hannah were friendly—Amanda referred to Mary as "my dearest chum"—but, try as she would, Mary had never felt very close to Mrs. White.

"My wife asked for you especially. She would welcome your help in the kitchen and with the children. Our three older boys are away at school, but she has her hands full

✹

with the two younger children, especially Mary Ann. She is just eight and needs a firm hand."

Mary could earn her keep. "Then I'll come, Mr. White. Tell Mrs. White I'd be pleased to help her."

On her arrival at the White homestead on Main Street opposite the Town Hall, she mused, "I'll have a home now and an adopted family."

"Did Mrs. Bascomb mind your leaving her?" Mrs. White wanted to know.

"Oh, no," said Mary, aware almost at once of the contrast between her own rough hands and homemade dress and Mrs. White's trim neatness. "Mrs. Bascomb doesn't mind. She never sees me anyway. She told the neighbors that I only sleep a few hours. You know what she asked me the other day?—why I hurried through my meals as though the Devil himself were after me."

Mrs. White raised her eyebrows. "Why, Mary, what a thing to say!" Mrs. White could see no humor in speaking lightly of either God or the Devil.

"You're to have the room with Amanda upstairs next to Hannah and Mary Ann." Hannah was a gentle, slender girl of twenty and Mary Ann, a real tomboy of eight. "And you're to help in the kitchen whenever I need you."

"You must do something," Mrs. White confided in her husband a few days later. "Mary is all intellect. She doesn't take care of herself properly and never knows what to say to our guests. Why, yesterday she just stood at the door as awkward as you please and said nothing to Mr. and Mrs. Little. I was embarrassed. And her clothes! She came without gloves or hat."

A NEW HOME

Mr. White laughed. "You tell her, Mother."

"No, I'll not. You're the one who asked her. You tell her." With obvious reproof, Mrs. White picked up her sewing and left the room. Mr. White knew he shouldn't have laughed. He supposed manners were important, even for a young student. Forced by his wife's insistence, he finally called Mary into his study and talked with her.

"Mary, this is the way you look when you walk," he mimicked. "This is Mary Lyon as she runs through the house."

Then they laughed, Mary at herself, and Mr. White because laughter brought understanding. Yet she realized that she would have much to learn to be a credit to Mrs. White.

She could never seem to manage to take time to put the dress collars on perfectly straight. And at the table she was always picking up the wrong fork or knife. At times it irritated her to be corrected in front of the children. Still, she was content in her "adopted home," mostly because of the children. In the evenings she often read aloud to them before bedtime, and whenever she was free during the day, she took them outdoors for long walks.

That first summer, Mr. White arranged for Amanda and Mary to go to summer school in Byfield, Massachusetts. It was a new school for girls that Joseph Emerson, cousin of the famous Ralph Waldo Emerson, had recently opened. But Byfield was a long distance from Ashfield, almost all the way across the state. It was more than a hundred miles east, near Newburyport, and about thirty miles north of Boston.

"Aren't you lucky!" Hannah cried. "Mother says I have to stay home and help her."

*

"I don't think I'm lucky, and you know it," pouted Amanda. "Mary probably thinks so, but not I. I wish you were going instead."

"I wish you were going too, Hannah," Mary interrupted. "But I think we are lucky. You'll like it, Amanda, when we get there."

As Mary read through the circular listing the courses—natural philosophy, rhetoric, history and geography, religion—she hoped she could do the advanced work. She wouldn't want to disappoint the Whites. She wondered why Amanda wanted to stay home. It wasn't like her not to be excited about a trip of any kind.

It would be a three-day journey to Byfield, and Mary had never been more than twenty-five miles from the farmhouse in which she was born. Here she was, traveling more than a hundred miles, all the way to the Atlantic Ocean! For Mr. White had promised them a side trip to Newburyport to see the harbor and the sailing vessels, some of which he said went around Cape Horn.

How little she knew that Byfield Seminary was to be a turning point in her life.

8
A TURNING POINT

Mary had expected Amanda to settle down happily after the long, hard trip east from Ashfield to Byfield. But to her surprise, the combination of living in a country farmhouse, taking care of her own clothes, and the muggy, hot weather constantly irritated Amanda. Not Mary. It was her first chance since the summer at Amherst to collect more plants and wild flowers. She sorted, pressed, and classified several new specimens found on walks to nearby South Byfield and Georgetown.

One afternoon Amanda came into the room while Mary was looking over the plants spread out on the table. "You've been poring over those for hours," Amanda remarked. "What on earth are you going to do with them?"

"I really don't know. I've done this for years—'weeds,' my mother always called them." She explained how a Professor Eaton at Amherst had shown his specimens of plants

※

to a class she attended, lecturing on the species that grew north of the Gulf of Mexico.

"Did you show him your collection?" Amanda asked with sudden interest.

Mary shook her head. "Oh, no. Mine is really a very small collection—and I've only got specimens from around Putnam's Hill."

But despite Amanda's apparent curiosity, she seldom went with Mary on these botanical trips. "I'd rather stay indoors," she'd apologize. "Look at me. I'm already covered with freckles from the bright sun."

There was something in the casual manner in which Amanda made her apologies that disturbed Mary. Amanda had been her best friend—there was no need for pretense. Yet somehow they weren't as friendly as they had been when they studied together at Sanderson.

One Friday Mary returned from school in time to meet the postman. She smiled at him as he pulled his horse to a halt and handed her the mail. There were two letters from Michigan, and the sight of William Ferry's neat handwriting was enough to make up for all the long weeks of waiting. She took the letters into the living room and curled up on the couch to open them.

Then she gasped audibly. One was addressed to Amanda! She placed it on the side table in the hall and went up to her room, where no one could see the trembling of her hands.

William started out by apologizing for not writing sooner, but he'd been busy with the building plans for a new church. He went on to mention the Indian children he taught and to tell how many of the women of the Chippeway tribes had been converted and joined the Christian church. He signed

A TURNING POINT

the rather short letter, "Love, William," but he said nothing about his return. Nor did he mention missing her.

Maybe he doesn't, Mary reflected, folding the single sheet of paper. Amanda, perhaps? The realization of this possibility hurt, but she pushed the thought away. Stuffing William's letter into her blouse pocket, she went downstairs and outdoors. An hour or two in the chemistry room might help. In any case, she quickly decided not to mention the letter to anyone, not even to Amanda. But she need not have worried, for Amanda never shared hers with Mary.

Even in the science room she couldn't keep her mind on her work. She knew too well that William had objected to her experiments in the laboratory at Sanderson. She finally admitted to herself that their only real difference had been over the conflict between science and the Christian faith. But it was a difference he had refused to discuss.

"You sound like a Unitarian," William had said. Unitarians professed openly disbelief in the doctrine of the Trinity, rejecting the divinity of Jesus and holding that God is a single Being.

"Maybe I am," Mary said, and the embarrassment she felt made her voice a little sharp. "But I don't call it unchristian to question."

William didn't answer, just sat there looking at her in a searching way.

"Anyway," Mary said, closing Paine's *Age of Reason*, "as Paine points out, I, too, sometimes feel God's goodness in the world around me—and I don't need the doctrine of the church for that."

"It's your right," William had said impatiently.

It *was* her right, she told herself. But just the same, it

✱

hurt a lot to find William unwilling to consider her point of view. She wondered if her letters had been too full of her own excitement over the work in chemistry and astronomy at Amherst and so had seemed unsympathetic. Letters could be so easily misunderstood. If only she could see him and talk with him. Another spring seemed years away.

Mary picked up the textbook and went back to her testing. She was mixing equal portions of cold and boiling water and measuring the heat of the mixture to determine temperature changes in cold, warm, and boiling water. A few days later she reported her experiment to the class at the request of Miss Grant, the senior teacher. Miss Zilpah Polly Grant assisted Mr. Emerson, hearing lessons and keeping the records. Mary had often admired her quiet efficiency, but felt slightly awkward in her presence. Stately and serious of manner, Miss Grant permitted no laxity in her students, and a flash of her black eyes or a frown was enough to prevent this.

The shrill sound of the school bell ending the class period brought the usual rustling of papers and closing of books. The girls waited for the signal from Miss Grant before leaving the room. Amanda and Mary were passing Miss Grant's desk when the teacher said, "Mary, I want to talk to you. Can you wait a few minutes?"

"Of course." Mary's voice showed her surprise. She turned to speak to Amanda, but she had gone.

Mary wondered what she had done. She had thought her report was complete and accurate. No one had reported any results that failed to verify her findings. Why should she be singled out?

"Mary," the teacher said earnestly, "I don't know how

A TURNING POINT

to tell you, but I have heard from other students about a matter that I think you should try to correct. You were here at the opening talks by Mr. Emerson, were you not?" At Mary's nod she went on, "And is it true that you are still spending some of the Sabbath day in study?"

"Yes, it's true," Mary quickly admitted.

Sunday at Byfield was strictly a non-studying day, and Mr. Emerson had made it very clear to all the girls that the day was to be devoted to church attendance and worship, the usual procedure in a Christian school of the 1800's.

"I wonder," Miss Grant said, "whether you can accept this regulation. Can you, Mary?"

"I'll try, Miss Grant. It just seems that there is so much to study and learn. I don't mean to apologize—I know I shouldn't have studied on Sunday—but I've missed a lot of schooling that the rest of the girls have had."

"Oh?" the teacher's voice sounded a little less severe. "I didn't know. But I'm not worried about your work. Your grades are high enough and I'm sure you could spare the time from your studies." And Miss Grant looked up and gave Mary a friendly smile.

"You will think about it seriously?" Miss Grant added.

Mary nodded. "Yes, I will. Thank you for telling me."

As Mary walked down the now empty hallway and out the front entrance, she suddenly thought about Mr. Emerson. What did he think of her? "I must talk with him," she thought. "I wouldn't want him to be disappointed in my attitude."

She wasn't to know until she had a school of her own that Mr. Emerson had said of her, "For mental power she was superior to any pupil I ever had in my seminary." She did

※

know, however, that she'd always remember his belief in the value of education "to fit one to do good."

"I'm not surprised," Amanda said later when Mary told her about her talk with Miss Grant. "You shouldn't be, either."

"Why, Amanda, how can you say that? I don't know how she knew, unless . . ." Mary looked over at Amanda and waited.

Amanda flushed. "All the girls knew you were breaking the Sunday rule."

The bell rang for supper and Amanda bounced off the bed and headed for the door. "Coming, Mary?"

But Mary shook her head. "No, you go along. I'll be there in a few minutes."

In the days that followed, with final examinations to prepare for, the incident was not mentioned again. And to Mary's complete surprise, a week later she received an invitation to tea with Miss Grant. It was a note inviting her to the Big House, a former meetinghouse that was now a dormitory for some fifty girls.

But the prospect of meeting Miss Grant socially and mingling with the girls, many of whom she didn't know well, filled her with alarm. Still, how could she refuse?

The tea proved a pleasant affair, and Mary felt especially grateful to Mr. White for his "private" lessons in manners.

"You must come again, Mary," Miss Grant had said. "We'll want to talk about finding you a teaching position in a seminary like this. You'd be very good, Mary. You have a real gift for giving clear explanations."

"Thank you, Miss Grant," Mary murmured. The words of praise made her feel self-conscious. Still, she was happy

A TURNING POINT

that Miss Grant had complimented her. "I'd like to come again," she said.

The opportunity came near the closing week of school. Mary changed rapidly into a freshly ironed gingham dress and pinned up her hair. Arriving breathless at the Big House, she hurried up the steps and down the hall to Miss Grant's room. The door was open. She knocked quietly and said, "Excuse me, Miss Grant. It's Mary Lyon. I have some news for you."

"Come in, Mary." Miss Grant motioned for her to sit down. "Tell me all about it," she added, closing the door.

It didn't take Mary long to explain the reason for her sudden visit. "I've a chance to teach at Sanderson Academy when I get back to Ashfield. Mr. White has been appointed Chairman of the Board of Trustees and it looks as though he convinced them to take me. The school isn't so advanced as Byfield, but it's growing."

"Is it something you really want, Mary?" Miss Grant asked eagerly.

"I think so. Still, the job is only part time—an assistantship, he says."

Miss Grant frowned slightly. "I had hoped we might have a place for you here—but tell me, why Sanderson, Mary? You might do better."

Mary glanced over at Miss Grant and felt the color flooding her cheeks. How could she know about William?

"Maybe because Mr. White has been such a help to me —my coming to Byfield and all," she said thoughtfully. "I live with the Whites, you know, and they have been like my own family. It just seems too good an opportunity to miss— to return to Sanderson as a teacher."

✽

Miss Grant smiled affectionately. "Then it's settled. It will be a beginning for you, Mary, but we'll miss you here." She paused slightly and added, "Perhaps you'll write us once in a while?"

"Yes, yes, of course, Miss Grant," Mary agreed enthusiastically. But suddenly she couldn't bear to think of leaving Byfield. Endings and beginnings! Would her life always be like this? "I'll write you often," she promised.

And so, that August, cheered by the memory of the summer term and the diploma she'd soon hang in her room in Ashfield, Mary watched the receding hills of Byfield. She was eager to share the news of her teaching with her family, and her thoughts turned homeward. She had heard from her youngest sister Freelove that Aaron would soon be making his first visit back to Massachusetts.

9

THE MORNING COACH
FROM ALBANY

It was a happy family that gathered at the Taylors in Ashfield on July 17 of 1822, to welcome Aaron from western New York. Mary thought it was like Thanksgiving—the long table piled with food and all her sisters home. Daniel and Lovina had driven over with their two babies just after breakfast, and Elisha and Jemima had arrived soon after with their five children. The house was alive with excitement.

"I wouldn't know you," Aaron had said, looking at his younger sisters, Rosina and Freelove. They had walked to Willard's Tavern to meet the morning coach from Albany. "I suppose I've changed, too," he added.

"I should say so," Freelove said. "I remembered you as much taller and not so . . . not so fat," she faltered.

"And not so bald," Aaron said with a chuckle. "But you, you're both much prettier than I remembered."

"And you're still a tease," said Rosina, shaking her finger

✳

at him. And Freelove added, "You'd better not be teasing—that's the first compliment I've had in days."

This lighthearted banter seemed to set the tone for the whole day, and there was much laughter. Mrs. Taylor bustled about, happily filling and refilling Aaron's plate. Mr. Taylor was delighted to hear about the West and made Aaron feel at home. "Your mother and I once talked about going out to New York State when your uncle left. But I'm not the farmer you are—and then, there were the grandchildren!" He looked admiringly at three-year-old Sarah, Lovina's oldest daughter, who was playing contentedly at his feet, and then at his wife. This second marriage had been a good one, and he was at peace.

"Is the country as fine as they say?" he asked.

"Oh, yes, fine rich ground," Aaron said earnestly. "And flat land that can be plowed easily. That's real country out there. You have to see it to realize why people stay, even though they miss the folks at home."

He proceeded then to describe the log cabin they had built with the help of a neighbor. He told how few families lived there—the nearest one a mile away—and they wished to build a school for the children.

"Ezra is nine this summer, and not a day of school yet," he explained. Mary was conscious that he was looking at her quizzically. She wondered if Nancy and Lucy would remember her.

As if he had caught the unspoken words, he said, "Lucy runs about like a little Indian. She's a real tomboy. But you should see the baby, Mary Mason, your namesake." Aaron smiled broadly. "She has your red hair, Mary, but otherwise favors the Alden side of the family."

So the first day passed far too quickly. Soon it was time for the children to be bundled off to bed and for Mary to return to her "home" at the Whites. "I'll walk down the hill with you," Aaron insisted. "It'll be good for me."

"Now, then," said Aaron as soon as they reached the road. "What about it, Mary? I didn't want to tell Mother right away, but I really came for you."

"For me, Aaron? Oh, no," she said. "You're not serious, are you?" Mary stared at her brother, unbelieving.

They walked in silence for a few minutes. "You don't have to come, Mary," Aaron said quietly, "but we need you, and I thought you would want to come. I always thought so and now . . ."

Mary couldn't speak for a moment. "You'd like Stockton, and we need a teacher for the children," Aaron said simply.

"Oh, Aaron," Mary gulped, close to tears, "I'm so sorry. Why didn't you write me? I had no idea . . ." Her voice trailed off.

"I guess I should have written," he admitted. His voice sounded strange. "I just thought you'd want to come."

"I don't know how to answer you," she said frankly. "I don't know what to say."

"Then don't give me your answer tonight, Mary," Aaron said. "Armilla knows I'll not be back on the next coach, and I could stay here for a few weeks if you decide to come with me."

"But you won't count on it, Aaron?" Mary asked hesitatingly. Aaron nodded, and she added, "I'll think about it."

That night she sat alone near the window that looked out onto the maple-lined street. She saw again her own mountain home and Aaron: Aaron starting the fire on a cold morning,

✳

Aaron quietly listening to her troubles, quick with sympathy and understanding. She knew he cared, knew how much, but what troubled her was the way he assumed she would have no choice, that she would unquestionably go home with him to Stockton.

Would he understand the sense of obligation she had to Mr. White and to Sanderson Academy? She wondered if he knew how the White homestead had become her second home, and that she had found real satisfaction in teaching at the academy. Somehow, deep inside, she knew he would understand. He alway had.

"You've made a place for yourself here, Mary," he said later. "I can see that. But there's a new life for you out west if you should ever change your mind." Aaron spoke so gently that before she was quite aware of what she was doing she had told him about William. "It may not seem a good reason to you, Aaron, but I just can't leave Ashfield until he's back."

"Yes, Mary, I know," Aaron had said, and Mary felt relieved. She was glad she had told her brother about William. And whatever doubts she had about the wisdom of the decision were resolved soon after Aaron had returned to Stockton.

"I'd like to try my luck in the West," Rosina had written. "I'll come in Mary's place if you'll have me. I can't spin or weave as well as she can, but I can cook—maybe some young adventurer will be pleased with a Massachusetts wife."

So Rosina, attractive in a new blue taffeta, her eyes as blue as her dress, boarded the Albany-Buffalo coach. She carried a copy of Mrs. Sarah K. Trimmer's *An Easy Introduction to the Knowledge of Nature* that Mary asked her to take to the children. And Freelove, at first distressed by the thought of the separation, smiled through her tears as the coachman turned the horses onto the highway.

For several weeks after Rosina's leaving, Mary waited impatiently for the arrival of another Albany stagecoach. As day after day went by and she had no word from William, her hopes for his early arrival began to dwindle. By the time of the first frost, she decided that he intended to remain another winter. "And yet," she thought, "he might come before school opens in October."

But he didn't, and Mary was back at Sanderson Academy a month later with a full teaching position. Mr. Cross, the headmaster, had promoted her to the head of the girls' section, with an increase that brought her salary up to twenty-three dollars for the winter term. It was a good feeling to know that she would be able to repay Mr. White on the Byfield loan.

Though Mary still lived with the Whites, she no longer worked for room and board. For Amanda and Hannah had finished their schooling and now helped at home.

"Besides, you need your time," Mr. White explained. "Teaching is a full day's work." Yet Mary enjoyed doing the dishes and often helped Amanda after supper.

"Has Mother told you the news?" Amanda asked one evening, setting the dinner plates away in the cupboard.

Mary looked at her, puzzled. "What news?"

"William is on his way back. He was in Buffalo when he sent the letter, and he says he'll reach Ashfield a week from Saturday."

William on his way back? She felt a rush of joy and gratitude. He was safe. "What good news!" Mary said.

✳

"He'd have been on an earlier stagecoach, but he missed the boat connection at Detroit," Amanda continued. "And Mother says we're to have a homecoming party."

It seemed to Mary that Amanda was as excited as she was about William's return. She prattled on with great excitement. "And Mother has promised me a new dress for the party. I told her I wanted a red silk dress with yards and yards of ribbon trim."

Mary smiled knowingly. Amanda welcomed any occasion for new clothes. "There'll be a lot to do to get ready, and only a week to do it in," Mary answered.

Taking off her apron, she hung it up quickly on the door and hurried off to her room, unaware that Amanda was as eager as she to be alone. Unaware, too, that Amanda had tucked a letter in the cupboard drawer. Amanda pulled it out and read the words she knew so well: "Dear Amanda, it will be so good to see you . . ."

10

A LOCKET RETURNED

The next morning Mary packed up the dress she had worn for graduation exercises at Byfield Academy, a soft white muslin, and went up the long hill to talk with Freelove, her twenty-one-year-old sister, who still lived with her mother. "I need your advice and good counsel," Mary said.

"Need my advice?" Freelove asked, drawing in her breath slightly.

Mary nodded and smiled. Freelove was relieved. For days she had worried about Mary, wondering if she had yet heard the local "gossip."

Perhaps it isn't true, Freelove thought; perhaps I misunderstood.

"It's William, Freelove. He'll be back next Friday," Mary explained, flushing slightly.

"Oh, you heard from him?" Freelove cried with delight.

"No, not really, Freelove, but Mrs. White did." She

noticed the anxious expression on Freelove's face and added, "That's all right. My letter will come soon. You know how slow the mails can be these days."

Freelove nodded. "And there's to be a homecoming party at the Whites. I need a party dress. Do you think this will do?" And Mary opened up the package and held up the white muslin.

"Try it on," Freelove urged, her gray eyes warm and gentle. "I'll lend you a green sash to wear with it—green is such a good color for you."

Freelove sat watching her sister change into the soft muslin. Despite her frank manner, Freelove said very little about herself or her desires. Several illnesses had kept her in bed for long periods of time. She had learned to accept the limitations and had grown patient and more steady.

"I don't know . . ." Mary said doubtfully. "Do you think it will do? I wish it were silk or had ruffles."

"Why, it's pretty, Mary, and better without ruffles. But if you'll leave it with me, I'll trim the throat with a piece of lace."

Mary suddenly caught Freelove around the waist and gave her a hug. "You're a dear to do it. I can never trust myself when it comes to fixing clothes. You know that."

Comforted by her sister's need of her, Freelove brightened. "I'm so glad he'll be back soon," she said. With Freelove, Mary didn't have to explain her feelings; somehow Freelove always knew how she felt.

For the next week the White household was busy from early morning till close to sundown. There was much to do if everything was to be ready for the party. The company parlor was readied with new linen curtains, the house scrubbed so clean that even the pewter plates seemed glossy. A dressmaker spent two full days cutting and sewing for Mrs. White and her three daughters. There would be new dresses all around—if ten-year-old Mary Ann could be persuaded to stand still long enough to be measured and pinned.

After the candles were lit, Mary usually stayed downstairs with the family until bedtime. But not this week! Each evening she went to her room as soon as the dishes were done, eager to mend and sew her clothes. One evening in her haste she left her copy of Dwight's *Geography* on the living room table. Putting on her slippers, she went down the back stairs into the kitchen to get it.

As she reached for the kitchen door, she heard Mrs. White's shrill voice saying. "What makes you think that Mr. Ferry is going to marry her?"

"Why, I thought he was courting her," Mr. White answered slowly.

"Surely you understand what I mean. He has been writing regularly to Amanda, and I want you to help him make up his mind to marry her. It will be a fine match."

"Why, Mother . . ."

Turning quietly, Mary hurried up the stairs. She snuffed out the candle and, breathing hard, pulled down the covers on her bed. For a while she lay rigid, almost numb with shock.

Why hadn't she known? Why hadn't she suspected all along that things were changed between them? She felt heartsick and bewildered. Probably everyone knew about William and Amanda. Did Freelove know? Why hadn't her sister told her? She recalled the letter from William to

※

Amanda at Byfield. Probably there had been others. And Mrs. White had talked of William often, and had received letters from him when none came for her.

She couldn't close her eyes. She got up and lit the candle, wrapped herself in a woolen blanket, and sat by the window.

Then her thoughts turned toward William. She realized how many things she had done because of her love for him. She had finally joined the Reverend Mr. Clark's church, the Congregational Church in Buckland—a missionary's wife would have to be a church member, she realized. But if she were honest with herself, she knew that she had done it mostly for William.

Suddenly she sat straight up. She knew what she must do.

On the evening of the homecoming party Mary waited in her room until it was time for dinner. Soon she knew by the sound of voices and the gay laughter that the guests had arrived. She placed a soft woolen shawl around her shoulders, opened the door into the hallway, and went slowly down the stairs.

As soon as she entered the parlor, she saw him standing near the spinet with a group of ladies. She hesitated for a moment. Then she turned and walked toward him.

"Welcome back," she said, holding out her hand.

Taking it, William looked at her searchingly and said in a low voice, "It's been a long time, Mary."

"Yes," she said quietly, "and has your work been . . ."

"So there you are," Mrs. White interrupted, slightly annoyed. "Come, Mr. Ferry, it's time for dinner, and Amanda is waiting for you."

With a look of embarrassment he bowed slightly, flushed,

and followed Mrs. White across the room. Mary felt the color returning to her cheeks. William looks well, she thought, but he seems older and sterner.

Sitting between Hannah and Mary Ann at the dinner table, she somehow managed to avoid talking with him. She chatted with the girls throughout the meal and, carefully controlling her voice, gave no indication of her feelings. But as soon as dinner was over she went into the kitchen and out by the back door. The cool air pushed against her and she walked briskly along the Buckland Road until she felt at ease with herself. Tired out at last, she slipped back through the kitchen door and went upstairs to bed.

The next morning, her mind made up, she walked over to the academy and went straight to Mr. Ferry's former classroom, where he had left his small library. It was Saturday, and she felt sure he would be there as he had often been in his teaching days. She paused a moment before the door and listened a while. Then she went in.

"I hoped I would find you here," she said.

Startled by her unexpected presence, William dropped the book he was holding and stared at her.

"I'm sorry," she said, "if I disturbed you, but I wanted to see you." She took from her bag the small gold locket and handed it to him. "Here, William. You'll want this for Amanda."

"But Mary," William explained, "I didn't mean it to be this way. It just happened. Believe me, Mary."

Mary shook her head.

"I thought you probably knew how things were when I stopped writing so often," he insisted. "Didn't Amanda tell you?"

✳

"No," Mary said soberly. "No, I've been busy."

"Yes, you were too busy," William answered. Mary detected a note of bitterness in his voice. She looked at his sober face and knew he meant it. There was nothing more for her to say.

He put the locket into his coat pocket and added as an afterthought, "You're a very successful teacher, Mr. White tells me. I wish you well in your teaching, Mary."

"And I wish you success in your ministry in Michigan," she said quickly, and walked away. As the door of the classroom closed, she felt as though she had left part of her life there.

That night she packed her things and prepared to take a room at Mrs. Houghton's lodginghouse on Elm Street. She could no longer stay with the Whites. Although she regretted leaving her adopted family—especially Mr. White, who never once had made her feel unwanted—she did not hesitate. It would be but a few months before the wedding.

Soon after the winter term at Sanderson Academy, Mary was offered a summer schoolteaching job in Conway, a distance of about seven miles east of Ashfield on the Amherst route. She accepted eagerly—anything to get away from Ashfield.

But the summer proved a happier one than she could have imagined. Mrs. Orra Hitchcock, whom she had known in her classes at Amherst four years earlier, invited her to stay with her and her husband, Edward Hitchcock, minister in the Conway Congregational Church.

Mr. Hitchcock used his spare time studying in the sciences and willingly tutored Mary in chemistry. With Orra she spent free afternoons drawing and painting.

"I never knew I could do so little with a brush," she told Orra. "Goodness, I'll certainly respect an artist after this experience." Orra was an able illustrator of books on nature.

"I think you're a scientist at heart, Mary," Orra comforted her. "And a teacher."

In late August, Mary returned to her teaching at Sanderson Academy for the third year, and there she might have stayed to teach for many winters if she had not been invited to assist Miss Zilpah Polly Grant in a new school for girls in Londonderry, New Hampshire. She was able to resist the offer by mail, but when Miss Grant herself arrived on the post chaise from Byfield, Mary decided to try her fortune in the new field of "female education."

11

A GREEN VELVET BAG

"I couldn't refuse Miss Grant. She was really persuasive. I told her I'd let her know soon," Mary confided to Freelove the next day.

Miss Grant had driven across Massachusetts from Byfield to ask Mary to be her assistant teacher at a new school in Londonderry, New Hampshire, Adams Female Seminary.

"What's to prevent you from going?" asked Freelove.

"Nothing, nothing, I guess," Mary answered. She got up out of the rocker and stirred the fire to a full blaze.

It was March, and still cold, with snow in patches on the ground from a fresh storm.

The room was silent for a while except for the sound of the crackling logs. "New Hampshire is a long way from Ashfield," she added.

Londonderry was somewhat farther than Byfield, more

than a hundred miles away and ten miles north of Nashua, a mill city on the Merrimack River.

"I know," said Freelove. "But with Miss Grant . . ." Her voice trailed off. She knew how much Mary had praised this fine teacher of hers at Byfield Academy and how much respect Mary had for her. She had told Freelove once that Miss Grant was all she wasn't—elegant and refined.

"Nonsense," was Freelove's immediate reply.

Mary told Freelove about Miss Grant's new school. "It's to be one of the few academies for girls and mostly for those who want to teach," explained Mary. She smiled and added, "—not one of those 'fashionable' schools where they teach needlework and china painting."

She hesitated a moment and added, "And my salary will be five dollars a week besides my board. I can even save money!"

"It sounds like a wonderful opportunity, Mary," said Freelove. "I think you ought to go."

Mary nodded. "I'm glad you feel that way."

One week later, Mary resigned from Sanderson Academy and wrote to Miss Grant, "I'll come to Londonderry in late April for the opening of the Adams Female Seminary."

When Sanderson Academy closed on April 5, 1824, Mary accepted an invitation to study botany and chemistry with Professor Amos Eaton, a free-lance lecturer at Amherst from Troy, New York, and a noted geologist. He had written her earlier about the "new college" in Amherst, founded in 1821, and had urged her to attend his lectures.

Besides, Orra Hitchcock had written, "We shall be at my parents' home in Amherst for the summer. Grandmother

＊

wants to see the baby. . . . Do plan to spend your vacation with us."

In the days that followed, Mary became absorbed in her new studies and in the experiments of Mr. Eaton.

"Mr. Eaton is a fine teacher," Mary told the Hitchcocks at dinner one evening.

"He's also a great scholar," said Edward Hitchcock. "After I heard him speak once, when I was principal of Deerfield Academy, I decided then and there to try my hand at the study of natural history and botany."

To many, Edward's strong interest in science seemed strange. It was unusual in those days for a minister to try to prove that the Biblical views of creation were consistent with the findings of the geologist. "Atheist" was a term easily applied to a liberal Christian.

Mary continued to enjoy her studies. She also enjoyed the evenings, talking over the day's experiences with Edward and Orra, and one whole day she and Orra spent shopping in Northampton, a small city seven miles south across the Connecticut River.

"Thoughtful Hannah White!" Mary exclaimed. "When I wrote her that I was going to teach in a 'select' girls' school, she asked her father to send me a few extra dollars. Now Mr. White writes that he has put forty dollars on credit for me in several shops in the city."

Orra and Mary shopped in all the stores on the list, spending the entire sum. Most of the purchases were for necessities. Except one luxury—a soft green velvet bag.

She didn't need it, and she might not have bought it but for Orra. "It's handsome, Mary, and just matches your gloves. Green is such a good color for you. And it will wear a long time—velvet always does."

It would have to do for a long time, too, Mary thought.

Happy and profitable as the two weeks had been, Mary looked forward to being with Miss Grant at the new Londonderry seminary. When the day for her departure came, Edward Hitchcock walked with her to Rockwood and Bolton's Mansion House and put her on the coach for Boston. "Make our home yours whenever you can, Mary," he said. And so she often would.

As the coach rolled along through the Barre Plains toward Worcester and Boston, she looked back over the events of the past weeks. She was twenty-seven years old and yet had never been made to feel out of place in her classes at Amherst. To her delight, she had found students of all ages, "from nine to thirty-two," she told Hannah White later, and from all parts of Massachusetts. She held the velvet bag carefully in her lap and pulled around her the homespun coat that she had made on her own loom.

She recalled, as she journeyed eastward, the day that Mr. Eaton had come into the laboratory when she was trying out an experiment to demonstrate the principle of air expansion. She had taken down from the shelf an oil lamp, a lamp furnace, and the necessary tubes and glass bulb.

"You're not going to have all this equipment in your lab at Londonderry," he commented brusquely. "Here, let me show you how to do the experiment another way."

He picked up a large bladder and washed it. Then, after blowing it up, he tied it securely at the mouth with a piece of string and held it near the flame of the oil lamp. The

✻

bladder burst with such a resounding noise that Mary jumped. He chuckled at her reaction and said, "I'm sure your students will remember this experiment."

He had promised to send her any apparatus he could later in the year, and as she rode along, she made out a tentative list.

Early in the evening of the following day, the coach from Nashua, New Hampshire, neared Londonderry. Mary turned her thoughts toward a "second Byfield," Adams Female Seminary.

"Call me Polly," Miss Grant said soon after Mary's arrival. "My name is Zilpah Polly, but I much prefer Polly. Do you have a middle name too?"

"Yes," Mary answered hesitantly. "I was actually christened Mary Mason, but I don't like my middle name and I finally even dropped the *M*. My mother used to call me Mary Mason when I had done something she didn't like," Mary confessed.

The first days seemed to fly by. Mary thoroughly enjoyed the busy life but it wasn't long before she realized that Polly was troubled. "It's not you, Mary," she explained. "It's the trustees. I keep getting pressured to spend less time on the study of the Bible and more on music and foreign languages. They knew I had a strong program in Biblical study at my other schools. I don't understand this change in attitude."

The trustees understood what Polly had refused to accept: that a new liberal movement in religion was affecting educational programs, and that parents wanted children to have less emphasis placed on the Bible and more attention given to music, dancing, and foreign languages.

It is doubtful that even Mary knew fully what was happening, although she had written to her mother about some of Polly's religious sessions.

"Imagine," Mary wrote, "a little circle of about forty females all appearing as solemn as eternity."

When Catherine Beecher, head of the Hartford Female Seminary in Hartford, Connecticut, offered Polly a chance to teach with her, Polly was sorely tempted. She told Mary, "Miss Beecher complains of the neglect of the moral and religious side of education. She reminds me that I should hold out against the pressures of the literary and scientific departments."

So Polly tried to hold out, and she continued to spend as much time on Bible study as she had planned. When the next term opened, she was notified by the trustees of an increase in salary. It would be $350 the next year, with an allowance of half the tuition fees for all students beyond the total of sixty-five. More than a hundred students had enrolled. It looked as though Polly's ideas were acceptable.

In August, during the vacation between terms, Polly planned to go to Boston to shop for school supplies. A slight attack of pleurisy, however, put her to bed, and Mary went in her place.

It proved to be an exciting trip for Mary, for on the two-day stay she had found time to visit a model school demonstrating the new Lancastrian method, introduced by Joseph Lancaster of England.

What intrigued her most was the idea that by using older pupils as monitors to teach the younger ones, the cost of education might be cut considerably. Why couldn't she and

✷

Polly try it at Adams? Had Polly really meant it when she said she believed strictly in classes of ten? "I'd have a tutor for each girl if I could," Polly had said.

Hanging her chintz shawl on a peg near the front door, Mary climbed the stairs to Polly's room. She knocked and entered, then sat wearily in the Carver armchair by Polly's bed.

"My, Boston is a busy place these days!" she began. She pushed back the red curls from her forehead and unfastened the top buttons on her shoes, looking at Polly.

"I found a few books we needed at Thomas and Andrews' Bookshop on Cornhill," Mary reported. "And I had time to go over to Harvard College . . . and to visit some public schools."

Then Mary eagerly told Polly about the large spelling class of more than a hundred boys and girls that she had seen. "One teacher taught the lesson first to a small group of ten older boys and girls," she said. "And they in turn taught the lesson to the younger children. You should have seen them, all standing in straight rows, working without a whisper. The monitors used charts and slates afterwards for reviewing in smaller groups."

"Do you really think they learned anything that way?" Polly asked.

"Oh, yes," Mary answered with conviction. "And I even think . . . if you would be willing to try . . . I think it would work with our seminary students."

Polly shook her head. "I'd want to know more about it before we tried it." She paused and added, "I guess you're braver than I am in making changes, but I think we had

A GREEN VELVET BAG

better wait a while—at least until we see how well it works in other schools like ours."

Adams Female Seminary closed its second term for the year in mid-November and wouldn't open again until April. Although some schools for boys continued throughout the winter, many families would not allow their daughters to be away from home during the winter months. Even in cities like Boston, girls usually attended school from April to November, and not during bad winter weather.

"If you want to reach me for anything," Mary told Polly on leaving New Hampshire, "I'll be at the Clarks in Buckland. Mr. Clark is the minister of my church there. I look forward to having a lazy winter."

But idleness was never a part of her life, and she soon grew restless. She joined the Benevolent Society of the Congregational Church and helped fill missionary boxes, knit socks, and went from house to house collecting contributions. She unpacked her books and wrote to Mr. Eaton for suggestions about studying. After receiving his reply, she felt even more restless.

"I have taken a new appointment as head of the Rensselaer School here in Troy," he had written. "We are planning to open a scientific school in April. Why don't you come and stay with us? Even if it's only a few weeks, you can study and then attend my lectures and I can tell you many things that may be useful at your Londonderry school."

What would she do in the meantime?

"Start a winter school right here, Mary," Mr. Clark proposed.

"Why, Mr. Clark, you're joking," she stammered.

✻

"No, he isn't," interrupted his wife. Mrs. Clark was the former Priscilla Williams, who had once studied with Mary at Sanderson Academy.

"No, I'm not," reaffirmed Mr. Clark. "We have both talked about this possibility for some time—ever since we knew you would be back here. Buckland girls have no school beyond the district school." He paused and then said quietly, "What do you say, Mary?" Then he looked across at his wife and smiled, "Priscilla says you're the best teacher she ever had. . . . But put on your coat and come along. I have something to show you, Mary."

Mr. Clark and Mary walked briskly down Main Street past Jones' country store and up a maple-bordered drive. They climbed the steep rise to the Griswold homestead, where Major Joseph Griswold lived with his wife. The Major had built the house in 1818, modeling it after a famous town residence he had admired as a young man.

As the Major opened the door, Mr. Clark said, "Mary Lyon and I have come to see the ballroom, Major."

"Come on in, Mr. Clark," invited the Major, a slightly rotund man with a round, merry face. "Come on in, Mary. It's good to see you."

They followed him into the front hallway, up the second flight of stairs, and into a long room that ran the entire length of the front of the house. In each corner was a small fireplace and on the east side two large windows. The walls were painted with country scenes, done by an itinerant artist. Mary stood enraptured.

With a flourish and slight bow, Mr. Clark announced, "There, Mary, there's your schoolroom—thanks to the Major."

A GREEN VELVET BAG

She gasped audibly. "My schoolroom?"

"Yes," said the Major promptly. "It's yours if you wish to use it. Room enough, I'd say, for a class of fifty girls."

"I . . . I don't know what to say. You are most generous. I had no idea this was your plan, Mr. Clark."

Mr. Clark and the Major said almost at the same time, "Do you like it, Mary?"

Mary nodded. "It's practically perfect."

"You will be doing Buckland a real favor," said the Major.

Few grammar schools were open to the girls of Massachusetts in the early 1800's, and there were no schools specifically for preparing teachers. There would not be a "normal" school for twelve years, when Horace Mann was to found the first such school in the state.

Academies were mainly for boys. In fact, the academy was New England's answer to the question of higher education for boys and, to a far lesser degree, for ambitious girls. In Massachusetts, Hadley, Monson, Andover, and Amherst were the four outstanding academies, but only Amherst was co-educational. And for poor girls, daughters of farmers like Mary, the schools were prohibitive in price. Mary wanted to correct this in her school.

Tuition would, she planned, be only three dollars for the winter term, and room and board would be from one dollar to a dollar and a quarter a week, depending on how much wood was used for fuel. No girl should have to pay more than twenty dollars a term, although even that might be hard for some to come by.

"I'll try out some of my ideas," she decided. "I'll teach geography the way Mr. Burritt did—with maps, and I'll

※

try out the Lancastrian method with my own students."

Four weeks later, just after Thanksgiving, Mary opened the Buckland School in Major Griswold's ballroom under the trusteeship of the Association of the Ministers of Franklin County. She rushed about happily as twenty-five girls came in from Buckland Center and from the surrounding villages —country girls like herself.

For the first time in American history a woman was conducting a school for girls of poor families, daughters of farmers and workmen. The day's planning and teaching kept Mary so busy that she had no time to realize the uniqueness of what she was doing.

In March, when the closing day of the winter term arrived, she packed her bags for a trip to Troy, New York, and the Rensselaer School of Mr. Eaton.

"I'll see you next winter," she promised the Clarks. "I have no further doubts, and the arrangement is just about perfect—a summer school in New Hampshire with Miss Grant and a winter school of my own here in Buckland. I have found my place at last."

From the broad valley of the Connecticut River, the Greenfield coach followed the Deerfield River into the Berkshires. As the coach wound its way through the mountain passes, Mary sometimes felt shut off from the world she knew. She tried to visualize how the Indians had broken the early trails. Then she thought of Aaron and Armilla, and sensed their feeling of pride in the West that Mary had never known.

THE MAJESTIC HUDSON

Although the long trip from Greenfield, Massachusetts, to Troy, New York, was a pleasant one, Mary was glad when the driver announced the arrival at Huddleston's House on River Street and saw the majestic Hudson, the great waterway of trade and traffic.

Anyone observing Mary as she stood looking at the Hudson River might easily have taken her for a pioneer on her way west. Sturdy and rosy-cheeked, she had the appearance of a woman who could face hardships—an assured, vigorous manner. Years later she would indeed be honored as a pioneer—in education.

"Beautiful view, isn't it, Miss Lyon?"

Mary turned quickly to see Mr. Eaton at her side, a smile of welcome on his heavy-set face. "This is Sally," he said, looking down at his eight-year-old daughter.

"Hello, Sally," Mary said. "Where are your brothers?"

✳

"At home, Miss Lyon." And Sally, with black hair and steel-blue eyes like her father, flashed a smile and curtsied. "Mother says I'm to tell you we're glad you could come."

"And I'm ever so pleased you wanted me," said Mary fondly. And taking Sally's outstretched hand, Mary followed Mr. Eaton across the street to a waiting carriage. Sally's brisk walk and manner reminded Mary of Aaron's daughter Lucy, and for a moment she wondered if she could ever persuade Aaron to send his girls east to school.

They reached the large homestead in North Troy in time for the noonday meal. Then Mr. Eaton drove Mary to the Rensselaer School, the first school of applied science, later to be the Rensselaer Polytechnic Institute.

Although Mary spent much of her time at the school attending classes in chemistry and natural philosophy and working in the laboratories, she took almost daily jaunts with young Sally.

"What are we looking for today?" Sally asked as they left the house, each armed with a pail and a basket.

"Today it's quartz," said Mary. "Your father said we might find some in the flats along the Hudson—Indian Fields, he called the place."

So off they journeyed. Sometimes they found what they were searching for, but more often they brought back stones that Mary couldn't identify or early spring reeds. The days were still cold and sharp, but Mary and Sally were content. "We're geologists," Sally told her mother.

Every evening Mary attended the courses in chemistry that Mr. Eaton taught. "It seems strange to call them lectures," she commented. "The students do most of the talking."

"I didn't realize you would find this procedure new, Mary," Mr. Eaton said. "Every student is expected to explain one experiment, and before commencement we require, as a test of qualification for teaching, several short experimental lectures."

"I think that's splendid! I never thought of it before, that's all." Mary looked up to see him watching her.

He chuckled and asked, "Does it make you feel less like a teacher?"

"No," she answered promptly, "more like one, I should say." She brightened and added, "But I told Miss Grant that I intended to go to your lectures. She'll be confused when I tell her there really were none."

Mr. Eaton's face took on a more serious look. "Tell her, too, that if she wishes to try this method—'radical,' some of my friends like Benjamin Silliman at Yale College call it—she'll need a great deal of equipment, a good library, and a well-stocked laboratory."

"I will indeed," she said. "You know, I'm constantly amazed at the amount of chemical apparatus and materials you have."

"Thank Mr. Rensselaer," he assured her. Mr. Stephen van Rensselaer had founded the school and had provided most of the money for buildings and equipment. He had also appointed Mr. Eaton to make several surveys, including the most recent one for building a canal to Lake Erie.

"Someday soon a canal will connect the Hudson River with the Great Lakes," Mr. Eaton told Mary. He stretched out a large map on the table in his office, and Mary eagerly followed his description of the rock formations and the geological profiles from the Atlantic to Lake Erie. He opened up for her horizons that she did not know existed, or had only surmised.

Here was a man who had risen above defeat. Falsely accused of forging papers in a real estate transaction, he had been sentenced to life imprisonment, to be cleared four years later through the intercession of the Governor of New York, De Witt Clinton. He had used the years to devise a new method of arranging species of plants and, freed at the age of forty, he had gone to Yale to study under the scientist, Benjamin Silliman.

Mr. Eaton reminded Mary of the religious zeal of Rev. Joseph Emerson of Byfield Academy. How alike they really were! Mr. Emerson preached the acceptance of the wonder of God; Mr. Eaton lived that wonder. Mary came to understand that Mr. Eaton was as much a man of God as any minister. It was a happy and acceptable thought. She couldn't be sure, however, that Polly would find the idea equally acceptable.

The afternoon before Mary had to take the coach back to Boston and to Londonderry, Mr. Eaton took her to visit the Willard School. Mrs. Emma Willard had opened a school for girls in Troy, which in a few years had become known as "one of the best female seminaries in the East." Mary had read her *Plan for Improving Female Education* and was most eager to meet her.

"You're ever so good to take me," she said, climbing into the carriage. "What is she like?"

"You'll see," Mr. Eaton said, picking up the reins. "And I really think you'll be surprised. She hasn't a 'no' in her vocabulary. When she was criticized for giving girls more schooling than they needed, she laughed at her critics."

"I suppose they said, 'But woman's place is in the home, and how will more education help women make better pies or darn socks?'" Mary commented, half in fun.

"Yes," Mr. Eaton said. "That's exactly what they said. 'And wouldn't higher education for girls upset the established order of things?'"

On reaching the center of Troy, they drove along the river and then turned into Second Street. Mr. Eaton pulled the horse to a stop in front of a yard full of laughing and shrieking girls.

Near the front door of the two-story brick building was a "candy woman" with a huge basket of goodies—taffy, peanuts, and chocolates. Girls were milling in and out of the building. Some were playing on swings and seesaws.

Could this be the famous Willard School?

"Yes, Mary," Mr. Eaton quickly assured her. "It's quite a different kind of school, but with all the freedom, the girls are good scholars."

Once inside, Mary was impressed. The building was as quiet within as the yard had been noisy. "The girls have a kind of self-government in this school," Mrs. Willard explained after the introductions were over.

If anyone could combine freedom and study, Mary felt at once that Mrs. Willard could. "She's both beautiful and persuasive," Mary wrote her sister Freelove.

Mrs. Willard's dignified manner reminded her somewhat of Mrs. White, but without her reserve and coldness. Mary was completely comfortable in Mrs. Willard's presence.

It was with great excitement that Mary told Mrs. Eaton

✷

about the visit at supper that night. "She certainly had courage. No woman before her ever dared petition a state legislature for financial aid for girls."

"Not only that," said Mrs. Eaton, "but when she said she'd close her school in Waterford, New York, if her plan was defeated in the New York State Legislature, she did just that."

When Mrs. Emma Willard closed the Waterford Academy for Young Ladies, a group of prominent citizens of Troy, New York, invited her to set up a school there. The city gave her a grant of four thousand dollars and offered her the free use of Moulton's Coffee House.

"An amazing woman," Mary stated.

"And charming," added Mrs. Eaton, sensing Mary's eagerness to understand this woman who had been able to secure the support of Governor Clinton and the personal encouragement of men like John Quincy Adams and Thomas Jefferson. Even two of Washington Irving's nieces had gone to her school in Troy!

As Mary journeyed back to Londonderry, she thought of her own school. How different! Even though Adams was an inexpensive school, it didn't have the social standing or prestige of the Willard Seminary.

She would have liked to discuss with Polly the possibility of introducing some phases of student self-government at Adams, but she hesitated to do so, remembering only too vividly the time she had mentioned Mrs. Willard's *Plan*.

"There must be some advantage in giving girls study in modern languages, music, and dancing," she had suggested. "Mrs. Willard . . ."

Polly had interrupted her. "Mrs. Willard. Nonsense,"

she said sharply, her dark eyes flashing. "I really don't care if she does get praise from the Governor of New York. What girls need today is more religious and moral training."

Mary talked very little about her visit to the Troy Female Seminary with Polly, but she wrote Hannah White, "I never saw so much material, globes and maps. The penmanship of the girls was truly remarkable. And do you know, every evening they sing and do some dancing, *'contredanse'* they call it."

Hannah had become a strong ally of Mary's, and the friendship made it possible for Mary to visit the White homestead again without bitterness. After a term at a school for girls in Wethersfield, Connecticut, both Hannah and her sister Mary Ann taught in the Ashfield district schools. Later, at Mary's urging, Hannah became an assistant and Mary Ann a teacher at the Buckland School.

Back at Adams Female Seminary in April, 1825, Mary's days were too busy to think further about the differences in the schools for girls. She had her work to do.

The enrollment at the Londonderry school had increased from sixty to over a hundred girls, and Polly had appointed two more teachers and a teaching assistant. It pleased Mary and Polly to see many of the first-year students returning for a diploma. They had decided to offer a graduating diploma to every girl who completed a full three-year course, hoping this would encourage the younger students.

Not only were the days busy, teaching and doing the hundred and one chores concerning meals and living, but visitors began to come. At first Mary and Polly were pleased by this, but after a while it was so time-consuming that they began to wonder what they could do about the situation.

✱

One afternoon, while Mary was sitting at her desk making out a shopping list, she heard the sound of a carriage coming up the drive. "Not another visitor," she said half to herself and, getting up, she went over to the window that looked out on the driveway.

It was General Derby from East Derry, a small town some three miles away. Whatever did he want? Calling to Polly, she hurried down the stairs and out the front door.

"He's coming the last of June, coming here," the doughty old gentleman shouted at them through his deafness. "I want him to visit our school."

General Elias Haskell Derby was still a spirited man who drove about in a handsome carriage, dressed as he had in the days of the Revolutionary War. For years he had worn an old blue jacket with epaulets and a three-cornered hat, a reminder of the months he had served with General Lafayette as a companion in arms.

"Who's coming?" asked Polly.

"Why, the Marquis himself—the great Lafayette," the General answered. "And you better have things in order, for I'll bring him around the last week in June. Here's his letter."

The General handed the letter to Polly and started to drive off, but held the reins a moment and smiled at the two surprised teachers standing in the doorway. "He's going to be my guest for a few days," he shouted.

"Why, I never . . ." said Mary as she watched General Derby drive down the hill toward East Derry. Of course, they had known about Lafayette's arrival in the spring of 1824. The papers were full of the triumphant tour he had made through the country with his son, George Washington Lafayette, his secretary, and a manservant.

City after city had vied to outdo one another in honoring him. In Roxbury, Massachusetts, just south of Boston, his own light infantry, wearing the familiar red and black plumes, had paraded for him. Wined and dined, he had met in Monticello the eighty-one-year-old Thomas Jefferson, and he had enjoyed a four-day visit with another former President of the United States, James Madison.

"But I can't believe it!" said Mary. "Visit Adams Academy?"

Then Polly read the letter. "He's quite right." She read aloud to Mary: "Dear General Derby, Mayor Quincy of Boston has asked me to lay the cornerstone of Bunker Hill Monument in Charlestown, the seventeenth of June. We plan to leave Boston for Andover and Concord on the twenty-second. I should be at your home in East Derry the following day and I'll stay with you a while. . . . signed M. de Lafayette."

Polly folded the letter and looked at Mary, excitement in her face and voice.

They hustled back into the schoolhouse and, without saying a word, Polly took down the bell from the shelf near her desk and rang it vigorously several times. It was more than an hour before the regular assembly time, but this news couldn't wait.

13

THE MARQUIS DE LAFAYETTE

For nearly a week, New England had been having its hottest weather of the summer. It was so muggy that Polly dismissed the girls from the class in calisthenics, allowing them to remain quietly in their rooms. Mary had hoped that the heat wave would end by the twenty-fourth of June, the day of Lafayette's visit to the school. But it didn't, and no rain came to relieve the humidity.

A few of the junior girls had gone out in the early morning hours to pick daisies, clover, and red Indian paintbrush and had put them into large pails of water to use for the ceremony. Then they made them up into individual bouquets.

"Look at these flowers," complained Eunice Caldwell, a senior, who had been put in charge of this part of the preparation. "They'll never hold up."

"Well," said Mary, a slight twinkle in the corner of her

mouth, "we may have to go flowerless." She added quickly, "Let's put them back into the pails and keep them in water until we're ready to go outside."

Heat and all, it was a busy morning and tempers easily became short. But everyone hustled about getting ready for the Marquis, who, according to General Derby, was expected at nine-thirty. There were books to be put in order, the hallway to be cleared of bonnets and shawls, and every girl was to be in the assembly hall at nine sharp, in white dress with pink ribbon sash.

As the girls entered the hall, Polly had them line up, a hundred and twelve in all, in four straight rows. "You are to take the same places in line when we go outdoors to greet General Lafayette," she explained. "There will be no talking, remember, and no moving about. We'll go out as soon as Dr. Dana gets here."

Dr. Daniel Dana, a trustee of Adams Female Seminary, formerly president of Dartmouth College, had taken a ministry in Newburyport, Massachusetts. Polly was pleased that she had been able to persuade him to drive the more than twenty miles to give the welcoming address. His arrival shortly after nine o'clock and his unruffled manner somewhat relieved the tension.

Mary picked up a copy of the *Memoirs of Lafayette* that she had purchased in Boston. Handing it to Polly, who was glancing nervously toward the door, she led the girls out onto the front lawn. And there they stood in five prim rows, each girl holding a small bouquet of wildflowers. No one spoke, but they looked across at the number of townspeople who had gathered to witness the event and waited.

Not a sound of horse or rider, and yet they waited for

✻

what seemed like hours. "Perhaps there is some mistake . . ." Mary offered. She had watched Polly's face grow flushed with the heat and noted its pained expression. Still, Mary hesitated to change any of the plans. The girls, too, looked hot and tired, and the flowers had long since wilted. It was a discouraged and unhappy group that waited in the heat.

Finally, Polly walked to the front of the group and began to read from the *Memoirs*. She read on and on. It was two hours before anyone spoke or moved out of position. At last, closing the book, Polly said, "We might just as well go inside for a while. Be sure to stay quietly in the assembly hall, for we'll come right out again as soon as we have rested a bit."

By early afternoon the girls and the teachers had reassembled. Still no word! All the townspeople had straggled off, disappointed in the delay, and even Dr. Dana had given up hope. He had just decided to leave for home when the whole sky suddenly darkened. Vivid flashes of lightning cut across the sky, with heavy and frequent claps of thunder.

Mary wrote afterward to Hannah, "The crashing thunder blanched many a rosy cheek and moistened many a bright eye."

What had been order became disorder. Without a command or directive, girls and teachers alike rushed for cover. It was a drenching downpour.

In the resulting confusion, no one heard the sound of the horsemen until they were almost at the entrance. One of the three dismounted and came to the door with the welcome news that Lafayette was on his way. "He'll be here in a few minutes," he called. "We left him just at the turnoff from the Portsmouth Road."

For the third time Polly and Mary reorganized the students. The long delay and the strain had resulted in some overexcitement and a few of the younger girls began to giggle. On the whole, however, the effect of the news was electric. The wet shoes and the faded flowers were forgotten.

This time it was a short wait, and then the Marquis de Lafayette appeared. Attended by four escorts, he entered just as a tremendous peal of thunder shook the building. But no one noticed the thunder as the great General came in. He was a sturdy old man, a little stooped and a little lame. But to Mary he looked as impressive as she thought he must have been as the daring young Frenchman fifty years before when, as a nineteen-year-old boy, he came to help George Washington.

With Dr. Dana, Mary and Polly went forward to greet the General and were introduced to him by his private secretary and assistant, Colonel Levasseur.

"We welcome you," Mary heard Polly say. "Our girls are most happy to see you here." Then, one by one, she introduced her students to him, and he shook hands with each, saying graciously, "I am happy to see you."

Mary watched the General, touched by the warmth of his personal greetings. She had read in a Boston paper that he had wept uncontrollably when he landed in New York Harbor the summer before.

She was equally touched when he bowed slightly, saying at the last, "Farewell forever." He lifted his plumed hat and waved. Following Polly to the door, Mary felt a sense of awe and reverence.

*

She would tell her students in the years ahead that she walked with Lafayette that day. Her own eyes somewhat dimmed with tears, she waved as the barouche, with its escort of four horsemen, drove away toward East Derry. Suddenly the thunder clouds disappeared and a rainbow crossed the valley. Off in the distance could be heard the church bells pealing the day's close.

Mary turned to dismiss the girls and saw Polly gazing at the west. "I guess," said Polly, "I don't need to say a blessing for this visit. The heavens have done it better than I ever could."

"No event during our teaching at Londonderry ever equaled the General's visit," Mary and Polly agreed years later.

Although Polly hoped that the trustees of Adams had been convinced of the need for religious training in her school, they continued to press their objections. And if Mary thought that Polly would accept the request of the trustees in the spring of 1827 to add music and dancing to the program, she was disappointed.

"I shall not consider it," Polly said bitterly. "When I came to Londonderry, the trustees agreed that one seventh of the time might be spent on Bible study."

"But the members of the Board have changed and new ones have been recently added, like Mr. Shepard . . ." Mary tried to explain. And she thought, times have changed. I'm no longer the stern Calvinist my mother is, and yet I don't believe in neglecting the moral side of education.

Polly sat upright in bed, where she had been for more than a week after a fall in the class in calisthenics. Troubles came in doubles. The pulled tendon would mean crutches for several weeks more.

The physical pain, however, was endurable. It was the personal affront that Polly couldn't cope with. "What will I do?" she asked Mary fearfully, handing her a circular that she had just received. It read:

FROM THE TRUSTEES OF THE ADAMS FEMALE SEMINARY

> It was the original design of the trustees to establish a seminary on liberal principles. We regret the institution has acquired the character of being strictly Calvinistic in religious instruction. This is in opposition to the sentiments and wishes of the majority of the trustees. . . .

Mary looked at Polly critically and leaned forward a little. "Does it mean . . . do you think they mean to close the school?"

"No," sighed Polly, wiping her eyes. "It's worse than that. I understand from Dr. Dana that some of the trustees are talking about having a man head the school because . . ." her voice was choked. She drew in her breath and continued, "because my usefulness is in question."

Mary had heard something similar, but had dismissed it as local gossip. Of course there had been criticism, but was there ever any progress without it? The school was a success, no matter what the trustees said.

"They asked my advice on the new courses," Polly admitted. "But I am sure from this circular that they have no intention of changing their minds."

"Maybe we might add some phase of music—vocal music, perhaps, and they'd . . ." Mary suggested.

✳

Polly shook her head. "No," she said firmly. "If I give in with one course, they'll try to force me to offer the course in dancing, and it's an evil I can't condone."

Mary remained silent for a while, not sure that her ideas could help. Mrs. Willard held singing classes, and Mary wasn't convinced that there was "evil" in either music or dancing.

A few weeks before the end of the term, the trustees voted to offer instruction in music and dancing at the seminary. The decision had been made.

"I have no choice but to resign," Polly sighed.

On January 7, 1828, Polly wrote to Mary, who was running her Buckland winter school, "I scratched with the goose-quill to inform the public that I was disengaged." She pressed the seal on the folded letter, picked up her crutches, and made her way painfully to the hallway where she laid the letter on the tray ready for mailing. No one, not even Mary, need know how defeated she felt.

Word of Polly's resignation soon reached the papers; less than four months afterward, she was offered the headship of a girl's school in Ipswich, Massachusetts.

Ipswich in 1828 was a thriving seacoast town on the Atlantic Ocean. Its ships were to be found in every harbor of the seven seas, and eight to twelve stages passed through the town every day en route from Boston to Newburyport.

"Come as soon as you finish your winter term," Polly wrote Mary enthusiastically. "The summer term will begin the 22nd of April, and Ipswich will be open all year. Must you continue teaching in Buckland, or can you close your winter school to teach in Ipswich Seminary full time?"

14

ON A CRUSADE

Brought up in the hills of western Massachusetts, Mary had never known the pleasure of living in a seacoast town. At Ipswich she could look across the sands and feel the salt spray on her face, and see the sloops and schooners sail in and out of the land-locked harbor.

One morning after church, Mary walked with Polly to the top of the rocky knoll called the Hill of Zion and looked down on the two-story frame schoolhouse, the Choate Bridge that crossed the river, and the mill beyond. "As soon as I can feel it is right for me, I'll close my winter school in Buckland and join you for the full year," she promised.

It was not until March of 1830, two years later, that Mary decided she could leave Buckland. It wasn't easy for her to give up teaching "her girls" in Buckland. She told Polly, "They are so easily guided. In scarcely any other place can I expect to feel so useful."

*

In the fall of the first term at Ipswich Seminary Mary had reason to question her usefulness if she continued in both schools. An attack of bilious fever left her weak. "My hair has come out in handfuls," she wrote Hannah. "I hope you'll recognize me in the turban I am wearing."

Sick again the next spring and suffering from headaches, Mary knew she would have to plan her life differently. Yet she was more concerned about her sister Lovina than about the Buckland School or her own health. Lovina had fallen ill after her husband's death and at times was disturbed and irrational.

"The best you can do now," the doctor finally told Mary, "is to put Lovina in a mental hospital. She may hurt herself or the children."

Daniel Putnam, her husband, had died the year before after months of illness, and since then Lovina had seldom left her room or taken much notice of the children. Once she had thrown a dish at eight-year-old Submit, her oldest child, and after that Freelove never left her alone.

"Poor dear!" Freelove said to Mary on her return from Ipswich. "She doesn't understand me at all. I'm afraid for her and, most of all, for the children."

So they agreed to send Lovina to the Hartford Insane Hospital in Connecticut, and Mary paid for the hospitalization and helped Freelove find foster homes for the younger children.

"There's no need for you to stay any longer," Freelove said firmly when Mary talked about Polly's plans for her at Ipswich Seminary. "You've helped all you can. And I shall take Submit home to Ashfield with me."

When Mary explained her decision to accept Polly's offer

to Mr. Packard of Shelburne Falls, chairman of the Association of Ministers of Franklin County, he was quite upset. "But we'd like you to stay here in Buckland and keep this school open all year."

"I know," she said. "The Association has been a strong support. I couldn't have continued without your help, and I am grateful."

"Then why not keep the school open all year? Your girls are needed as teachers in this county," Mr. Packard insisted.

Mary looked up and frowned. He was a difficult man to refuse. He hadn't mentioned the detailed letter she had written the Board, telling her reasons for leaving.

Hesitatingly she said, "I'd like to stay, but I can't, Mr. Packard. I have promised Miss Grant I'd teach summers at Ipswich Seminary as long as she wanted me, and it has become impossible for me to continue working in two places so far apart."

In March of 1830, she closed the Buckland School. For the next two years, Mary remained at Ipswich Seminary full time, first as an assistant teacher and later as co-principal. And this might have been the arrangement for many more years, but forces were at work in the life of the nation that were bound to have their effect on education— and on Mary.

It was the period of national awakening, with the development of waterways and highways, the beginning of railroads, and the sound of the machine. Andrew Jackson, a Democrat, man of the common people, became President of the United States.

In education, the public tax-supported elementary school

came into its own. Although schooling beyond the first six grades felt the effects of the changing social and economic forces more slowly, more older boys and girls were going to school and more private academies and seminaries were opening. Applications for enrollment at Ipswich Seminary increased beyond Polly's expectations, and soon Polly and Mary lacked adequate classroom space and sufficient equipment.

"Perhaps this is the time to think seriously about organizing this school the way colleges are set up for men," Mary proposed one evening. She glanced over at Polly and said, "I know the idea didn't appeal to you earlier . . ."

"It does now, though," Polly stated quickly, crossing the room to the table where Mary was checking over a list of schedules. "I hesitated at first because the trustees seemed so lukewarm about the idea."

Mary had hesitated too, because Polly hadn't fully recovered from an infection.

"There'll be a lot of convincing to do, Polly," Mary said slowly. They both realized that Catherine Beecher had been unable to secure additional support for the Hartford Seminary, even when she used women to convince the public of needed buildings. "Perhaps," Mary had said, "we should try to appeal to the men in the community."

It was finally the almost overwhelming problem of housing the girls that led to the proposal. "The teachers spend too much of their time in securing and supervising homes for the girls," Polly complained. "We simply can't accommodate more than a hundred and fifty girls, and we have over three hundred applications."

On February 7, 1831, Polly and Mary sent a joint letter to

the trustees, proposing permanent endowment through pledges and grants, and listing the building needs: a larger seminary building with a library, another laboratory, a reading room, and a boardinghouse for at least a hundred girls plus a few acres of playground space.

But April came and the school reopened without any favorable action by the trustees. Polly was forced by ill health to leave New England. "Dr. Warren says it's probably the result of my fall in Londonderry," Polly sighed.

Her injured leg had been put in a splint and for weeks she was confined to her bed with a diet of twenty ounces of food a day. But the leg didn't heal and Polly's strength was obviously weakening.

"He's wants me to go where it's warmer for a while," Polly said, staring down at her empty hands.

So, with a friend, Mrs. Briggs of Dedham, as a traveling companion, Polly went south and spent many months on a plantation in Savannah, Georgia. During her absence Mary ran the school with the assistance of Eunice Caldwell, a young teacher who had studied with Mary and Polly at Adams and had been a member of the first graduating class at Ipswich in 1829. Eunice had left Adams with about forty other pupils when the new principal took over the headship —it was a common practice in the 1800's for pupils to follow their teachers rather than remain with the school.

Mary sent a letter to Polly every week, keeping her informed of the news of the school and its special activities. She could not, however, bring herself to trouble Polly with her own grief. Within six months after Polly's departure, Mary had lost two of her sisters—Rosina, whom she had helped bring up at the mountain home, died in August, leav-

✻

ing four sons. And a month later, in Hartford, Connecticut, Lovina passed away in an epileptic seizure.

"Lovina would never have been fully well, I know," Mary said to Eunice, "but Rosina! It breaks my heart."

"Please ask Submit [Lovina's daughter] if she would like to come and live with me," Mary wrote Freelove at once. "Tell her I'll take care of all the expenses for her schooling at Ipswich Seminary."

A few months later Mary sent word to her niece Abigail, Electa's daughter in Fredonia, New York, "Come here to school when you're ready. . . . Your tuition will be twenty-five dollars a year, which I will pay with no personal obligation except that in Hebrews, chapter XIII, verse 16. Abigail took down the family Bible from her mother's dresser and, locating the passage, read aloud:

"But to do good and to communicate forget not;
For with such sacrifice God is well pleased."

That same year Mary proposed a new plan to the trustees of Ipswich Seminary but they voted it down. They couldn't be persuaded that it was sound to run a girls' school like Amherst College. It was financially too risky.

But the idea seemed right to Mary, and timely. In her business dealings at Ipswich Seminary, she had realized the weakness of private management. "I want a school that will outlive the teachers and the principal," she wrote Hannah. "I want a seminary that will not depend on individual whims or the chances of the time."

She finally explained her plans to Eunice Caldwell one afternoon. "I'm setting up a proposal for a seminary of my own," she told her.

"Without Miss Grant?" asked Eunice, looking up from her reading, a tone of disbelief in her voice.

Mary nodded, placing a pile of papers and accounts to one side. "I haven't been able to interest Miss Grant in leaving Ipswich."

Eunice looked puzzled. An unusually attractive young woman, Eunice reminded Mary of Polly when she had first known her at Byfield. She was as serious of manner and as sensitive.

Handing Eunice a large sheet of paper, she said, "I've changed my plans several times. This may not be the final copy, but I'd like you to look at it."

Mary was silent for a while as Eunice read. Slowly but surely, Mary's determination had grown. She would write out plans for a seminary for girls preparing to teach, but not for the well-to-do. This school would be for girls from places like her hills in Buckland, girls who couldn't afford the expensive education of a seminary like Ipswich or Troy. Mary knew full well the need in New England for women to have an education as broad and thorough as that furnished boys in the colleges.

"This is to be in New England?" Eunice questioned.

"Yes," Mary answered. "I'm calling it the New England Female Seminary for Teachers. But it will be a school that will ask no special favors of the town in which it is located. It might even be right here in Ipswich."

Eunice continued to look over the papers. Finally Mary said, "Wouldn't you like to join me in this strange adventure, Eunice?"

Eunice nodded her approval and said, "This will take time, perhaps a year or two."

*

Mary agreed. "Yes, even two or three years. I'll have to take that into consideration, but I'm going ahead on my own. I've written my decision to Miss Grant."

She had written it at the cost of some sadness and heartache, for they had started out their work at Ipswich Seminary with hopes that it would become a permanent school of high order and that it would be to young women what the college was to young men. She wrote:

> Ipswich, March 1, 1833
> ". . . but my thoughts are turned toward the middle classes of society. For this class I want to labor and for this class I consider myself peculiarly suited to labor. . . . I shall soon be forty years old; and if I am ever to leave my present field of labor, and begin entirely anew, it seems desirable that I should begin soon. . . ."

Mary got up slowly from her chair. It was a dreary day, chilly and rainy. She walked over to the hearth, poked the logs in the fireplace, and then turned to look out the window. She thought of her schooling, the days at Sanderson and Byfield, and said, half to herself, "I'll go west and see what the schools are like there. I'll go to Detroit. Maybe I should open my school in the West—in pioneer country."

Coming back to the desk, she sat down again and wrote to Electa: "You know, it's strange. Suddenly I feel like a crusader."

15
A TRIP WEST

"I may find more enthusiasm for education . . . and probably less criticism," Mary told Eunice as she packed her valise for the long trip west. "I'll go at least as far as Detroit if my money holds out."

Mary laughed lightly, but Eunice knew how much she had been disturbed by recent objections to her ideas on women's education.

"The only respectable education for women must be expensive," one of the trustees had insisted. "And they don't really need so much book learning as men. I still think Ipswich would be well advised to offer more female courses like French, needlework, and instrumental music rather than so much science and arithmetic."

"And this in the nineteenth century!" Mary had told Eunice, her voice high. "I couldn't convince him otherwise."

Her bag finally packed, Mary wrote in the long bound

✱

notebook she had bought for the trip: Cash Accounts—money on hand—$419.13. Then she made out a list of chemicals and apparatus she would purchase in Philadelphia and the schools she would visit.

"I'm going to Philadelphia first after I leave New York," she said as she outlined her journey. "I want to see Peale's Museum. Mr. Burritt wrote that it was well worth a special trip. It's the only museum of natural science in America. And I'll visit Miss Whitall's School and the Female Academy."

Her list for visiting schools and former students was a long one. She had helped place more girls in teaching positions than she realized. She had most recently heard from Grace Jeppon, a former student teaching in Detroit. "The demand is greater than you can imagine. If only you could come and see."

"I'll see Aaron and Electa, too, and the children," she added joyfully. "I haven't seen my oldest sister since she was married, and there are all my nieces and nephews, and other relatives . . ." Her voice trailed off. She'd miss Rosina. She never quite accepted the loss of this gentle sister whom she had helped bring up at the mountain home.

On the Fourth of July, 1833, at about five in the morning, Mary boarded the stage at Boston. Her letters told of the boat trip from Norwich, Connecticut, to New York, and then to Philadelphia by stage, railroad, and steamboat. "I closed the week," she wrote Eunice, "in fine health, except some little suffering in muscles and sinews."

She had visited the Peale Museum, advertised as the "seventh American wonder," not once but several times, and Washington Hall, where she was fascinated by the "Panorama of Mexico," a celebrated painting of the oldest place in America. She shook hands with President Jackson in Independence Hall, went to the navy yard to see the great ship *Pennsylvania* in drydock, and toured the United States mint.

"And I have purchased scientific equipment at Perkins Supply House," she wrote Polly. "I selected a half dozen Wedgwood evaporating dishes and a Gahn's blowpipe and some chemical supplies."

Mary had found it difficult to make the choices, and went back a second and a third time. There were so many pieces she had never seen before. She would have liked to buy more supplies but she had already spent over $130. If I spend much more, she thought, I'll not get to Fredonia, New York, let alone Detroit.

That evening in the boarding house she carefully set aside the price of coach fare to Fredonia and for the steamer up Lake Erie. She'd have almost a hundred dollars left, and, if she were economical, enough to travel up the Hudson, to spend a few days in Buffalo, and to see Niagara Falls.

She was able to do all that and more. She sailed on a steamer up the Hudson, admiring the unanticipated grandeur of its palisades, stopped at the Mountain House in the Catskills, and rode by stage from Albany to Troy to call on the Eatons and Mrs. Willard. Then she left for Buffalo, stopping several times on the long journey across upper New York State.

From Ithaca, she rode over to Clinton to attend the commencement at Mr. Bollett's School. She attended the anniversary of the Theological Seminary in Auburn, and spent a full day in Geneva Falls.

"Mr. Tyler and I talked a long time about female education," she wrote home. "We agreed that women should be well educated today, that the times needed educated women as well as men."

Then there was Buffalo and finally the great Niagara Falls. She would never forget this breathtaking sight, "the voice of many waters." She wrote in her notebook how she visited both the American and the Canadian sides during the day and then saw them again by moonlight. "I left," she wrote, "feeling like . . . a hungry man who is down at a table covered with richest dainties and just as he begins to taste is driven away to return no more."

It was the first week in September before she arrived at Electa's home in Fredonia, New York. Within a few days Aaron and his family drove down from Stockton to welcome her. Freelove was with them. She had gone out the month before to surprise her sister. It was truly a happy reunion.

"Are you going to stay here with Electa?" Mary asked Freelove. "You could help your sister with the children." Mary looked at her sisters and then at the two six-year-old boys, Electa's only son, Mason, and Stukely Ellsworth, Rosina's youngest boy, whom Electa had "adopted" after his mother's death.

"Electa has almost persuaded me," Freelove answered and flashed a bright smile at her sister.

"And you, Mary? What are you planning to do in the West?" Aaron asked.

"Are you going to teach out there, Auntie?" Abigail asked. Abigail, Electa's oldest daughter, was nearly twenty years old. She had finally persuaded her mother to let her go east and study at Ipswich Seminary.

"No," Mary said. "Just going to take a look for myself.

I guess you might say I'm the curious kind." Mary laughed, but Freelove frowned and looked disturbed.

"What's wrong?" Mary asked. "Why shouldn't I go?"

"Don't you know?" volunteered Aaron. "There have been some bad fires on the boats and several people have been drowned."

"I'd be afraid to go on a steamboat up the lake," interrupted Freelove.

But Mary went, driving the first fifty miles south with Electa in a small carriage. "I'll see you within two weeks," she assured her sister when she left her at Erie, Pennsylvania. After visiting the Pike School and Mrs. Chapin's School in Madison, Ohio, Mary took the lake steamer at the Fairport Dock. It was an overnight ride and she rose early to watch the sunrise and stood ready at the railing when the steamer docked. She looked across the lake, wondering if she might decide to begin her own school in this part of the country.

Others had done so. She thought of Edward Beecher, Catherine's brother, who had resigned his comfortable pastorate at the Park Street Church in Boston to go as president of the new college in Jacksonville, Illinois. "The college boasted only one small brick building on the outskirts of a little log-cabin village of the western prairies," Mary had heard him tell a missionary group on one of his return trips east to raise money.

Mary admired this young man. "He has the qualities of a true Christian," she believed. Now she wondered about herself. And for just a fleeting moment she thought how different her life might have been had she come ten years earlier.

✷

Perhaps Detroit would be her city. She had liked Buffalo, a rapidly growing business town that would "exert a vast influence during the next half century." Yet she was amazed at the need for good teachers and she thought for a while of the real possibility of beginning in this lake city. But she questioned the wisdom of it in the face of the instability she felt, a kind of unsettled feeling, as though she didn't belong.

Detroit proved disappointing. Hardly more than a military post, it was a dusty town in the full swing of emigrant travel. Wagons, coaches, and horse-drawn vehicles of all kinds moved in and out along the lakefront.

Still, it wasn't the dust or noise that troubled her. There were many fine homes beyond the docks, stores that reminded her of the East, and schools that were the equal of Ipswich. What more could she have expected! "Perhaps," she thought, "my roots are too deeply planted in the East."

For the next three days she would have time to find out. She would call first at Miss Jeppon's School.

"Miss Lyon, is it really you?" Miss Grace Jeppon hugged her teacher and cried a little. "It's ever so good to see you. When did you get in and where . . . ?"

"Wait a minute," interrupted Mary. She smiled and said, "I came in this morning and I'm staying at Mrs. Devaun's on Main Street."

"It's Miss Lyon, the principal of Ipswich Female Seminary and my dear teacher," Grace told her assistant, Miss Stevens. To Mary she said, "You must see the Colonel. He'll want to talk with you."

Colonel Lorner was one of the directors of the school and when he heard that Miss Lyon might be in Detroit at the

A TRIP WEST

end of the summer, he had told Miss Jeppon to let him know as soon as she arrived.

"He wants to open an advanced school and has influenced several of his fairly wealthy friends to join him," Miss Jeppon explained.

That evening and the next, the Colonel and several gentlemen, Messrs. Hastings, Jones, and Bates, tried to convince Mary that she should accept the principalship.

"I can't," she told them finally, "but I can help you get the teachers you'll need."

She tried to explain as tactfully as possible that she didn't favor "mixed" higher schools.

"But most of the academies here in Michigan and throughout the West are for both boys and girls," Mr. Hastings explained.

"And I hear that a co-educational collegiate institution has just been opened in Ohio—Oberlin, I believe," commented Mr. Bates.

"Yes, I understand," said Mary. But her school would be for girls. Mary wanted a school for middle-class girls, one that would be much less expensive than most seminaries. She knew now that she wanted to go back to Massachusetts to establish her "college."

The decision had finally been reached—she knew what she really wanted to do.

Boarding the steamship late that afternoon, September 21, Mary stayed on board watching the deck hands loosen the cables. As the boat sailed from the dock and the water grew rough, she picked up her valise and went down to her cabin.

She wrote in her notebook, "The *George Washington* is

✻

the largest boat on Lake Erie, a splendid boat 186 feet long, and carries 605 tons, almost 200 tons more than the Liverpool packets."

Back in New York, she stayed the first few days with Electa, returning to Stockton at the end of the week.

"They'll need more teachers, but . . ." Mary started to explain to her sister.

"But you're going to open your school in the East? Is that it?"

"Yes, somewhere in New England," Mary said firmly. She watched Electa washing the breakfast dishes. A large woman, she had grown quieter and more serious since her husband's death nine years before.

Electa knew now that there was no chance that either Mary or Freelove would stay with her.

By the first of October, the two sisters drove to Stockton, and there Mary left Freelove with Aaron and his family.

"I'll be home for Thanksgiving," Freelove had told Mary.

"And I'll come as soon as you open your school, Auntie," Nancy, Aaron's oldest daughter, promised.

"I'll come too," agreed Lucy, following her sister into the kitchen. Though two years younger than Nancy, Lucy was the more active and energetic. She looked like Mary at sixteen.

Mary had been back in Ipswich less than a week when she set her mind to planning for her "college." She spent every free moment trying to figure out ways to get support, as she later said, "from the hearts and purses of the friends of universal education."

She sent out a circular describing the proposed seminary

to all her friends in Ipswich and neighboring towns. And she sent copies to friends in Ashfield and Amherst. To the Hitchcocks she wrote, "If the church would do the same for young ladies that it has done, and is continuing to do, for young men, the work would be accomplished."

She wrote to Mr. Packard and asked if the Association of Ministers would help. She didn't leave a stone unturned. The months were busy ones.

"I am not proposing a church school," she made clear as she wrote her letters. "Rather I want the support of Christian people—I want a seminary like Amherst College or Harvard."

Mary had also not proposed an expensive school, but one with board and tuition at cost. "I plan to have the housework, the cooking, and the housekeeping done by the students. I really want a school that all girls can afford, but there's no hope of getting it without the support of the public," she explained.

The first objections to her proposal came unexpectedly from Catherine Beecher, a teacher in Ohio, whom Mary had known in the days when Catherine had her own private school for girls in Connecticut, the Hartford Female Seminary. Catherine had written a great many education books, including an arithmetic for beginners, and Mary admired her ability. Although twenty years later, in 1852, her sister Harriet Beecher Stowe would outshine her with the publication of *Uncle Tom's Cabin,* in 1830 Catherine was the writer of the family.

Mary told Eunice, "Catherine objects to the low tuition and the low teachers' salaries. Imagine, she writes I'll not get qualified teachers unless I pay more rather than less salary."

"How else can you operate at a low cost that all girls can afford?"

Mary shook her head. "She suggests that I give loans to students who can't afford the usual seminary fees or offer a combination of tuition and free room rent, or the like. But most of the letter is taken up with an idea of her own—that Polly and I help her financially to publish textbooks."

"For whatever reason?"

"Listen to this," Mary read from the letter. " 'Money is the sine qua non. Vast profits can be made by textbooks.' " Catherine had described the profit that was possible and wrote that Mrs. Lincoln had made over seven hundred dollars a year on her botany texts.

Yet Mary would not be discouraged, not even by Catherine's doubts. She continued to write and to plan for the seminary that was to serve all New England, not just her own Massachusetts. But as the months passed, it became clear that the hoped-for support and backing were not forthcoming. It was a bitter disappointment.

For two years she had spent time thinking and planning. To what purpose had she drawn up and altered plans, written and rewritten? If only she could have persuaded educators in at least two or three states to join together. Perhaps the proposal to have twenty-five men from different parts of New England appointed as a board of visitors was too ambitious a beginning.

How else could she establish a school that was not parochial, one that would serve the nation and be central for New England? Finally a possible answer arrived.

"Why not settle in the Connecticut Valley and work with a group of Massachusetts leaders?" Mr. Packard wrote at last in answer to Mary's earlier request. "I'll be in Boston on May 25 and 26. Can you plan to meet me one of those days at the Tremont House near King's Chapel? . . ."

16

BREAKING GROUND
AT SOUTH HADLEY

When Mary returned from Boston, she was pleased to see her niece Abigail waiting to meet her at the coach tavern. Abigail Moore, Electa's oldest daughter, had come east to study with her aunt and had stayed to teach at Ipswich Seminary.

"Just like your mother," Mary exclaimed. "Always so thoughtful." They climbed the hill together, Abigail eager to hear about the outcome of the meeting with Mr. Packard.

"Is it good news, Auntie?" she asked, walking quickly to keep up. For Mary, though slightly stouter than in her younger days, was still sprightly.

"Yes," she stated firmly. "It's not just what I first planned, but the arrangements look promising."

"Then you'll have your seminary soon?"

"I think so. Maybe in time for you to teach there, once you have had some experience."

"I'd very much like that, Aunt Mary," Abigail replied.

The next morning at breakfast Mary shared the news more fully with Eunice. "You won't believe it. I can hardly believe it myself. Mr. Packard will ask for a vote of approval from the Massachusetts General Association of Ministers. He's certain it's a mere formality."

Then she smiled in reminiscence and added, "He's forgiven me for leaving Buckland and says he likes the plan I set up. He will help me get started, and says he'll even come to Ipswich to meet with me."

Mary had proposed that the seminary should be located in Massachusetts wherever it seemed most favorable for raising the necessary funds, and that funds should be secured on a volunteer basis in the same way as was done for missionary work. Most important of all, she thought the money could best be raised through small donations by the middle class.

"Not the rich and not the poor," she has told Mr. Packard. "I've come to believe that the middle class contains the mainsprings and the mainwheels which are to move the world."

"I'm sixty-five years old," he had said in reply, "and too old to do much, but I'll do the little I can at the outset and someone else must carry on."

"Who that someone else is to be is a question," Mary told Eunice. "But I'm not worried." She smiled brightly. "I couldn't ask for a better friend than Mr. Packard."

"Did he approve of asking the Essex County Teachers' Association to open the drive for support, as Mr. Hitchcock suggested?" Eunice asked eagerly.

"No, he said there'd be too much talk and too little action. He suggested calling together a few friends of education."

※

"Why, that was your own idea," remonstrated Eunice.

"Yes, except when I last talked with you about a committee, I considered having women as well as men on it."

"Won't you be on it?"

"No, but . . . of course, I'll sit in on some of the meetings."

"But not as a voting member?"

"That's right. Men must take the lead in this undertaking if it is to succeed. I'm convinced of this, Eunice."

Mary held firmly to her belief in the value of "keeping in the background." She well knew it might be easier to do the work herself, but she also knew that the public wouldn't support a woman.

"They would think I was trying to make a name for myself," she explained.

On September 3, true to his word, Mr. Packard arrived in Ipswich to go over preliminary details. Although he favored having the seminary located in Amherst, he agreed with Mary that they should accept the decision of the committee.

"Meanwhile we want to consider the finances," he said, "and we must think about ways of raising money—how much we need to start, how much for buildings and the rest."

"I'll try to raise the first thousand dollars here before I leave Ipswich," Mary proposed. "I think I can do that. I actually have three months of the school year left. But we'll need more than that to get the location settled and to build the main building."

"It looks to me," said Mr. Packard, hesitating slightly as he looked over the records and papers he had brought with him, "it looks to me as though it would take between fifty and sixty thousand dollars in all."

Mary looked troubled. "We'll need all the help we can get, Mr. Packard."

At the Saturday meeting, Mr. Packard made his report on plans and finances. Only six of the dozen men who had been invited to the meeting attended, but they were men whose names would stand high in the years ahead: Mr. Daniel Dana, Mr. Edward Hitchcock, Mr. Joseph B. Felt, Mr. George Heard, Mr. David Choate, and General Asa Howland. As a result of their willingness to act, September 6 was to become known as "the beginning of Mt. Holyoke College for Women."

The Committee of Seven organized itself as the responsible agency to appoint trustees and to serve as directors until a charter was obtained. As elected chairman of the committee, Mr. Packard was granted permission to appoint a business agent to assist Mary.

"I shall ask Rev. Roswell Hawks of Cummington," he informed Mary after the meeting, "if that is all right with you."

The green velvet bag ever beside her, she knocked on any door where she might hope for a donation. Sometimes she traveled alone, but more often she was accompanied by her business agent, the Reverend Mr. Hawks. He had given up his parish in Cummington, a small town outside of Pittsfield, Massachusetts, to devote full time to the seminary. There had been some opposition to this, some of his parishioners saying he "must be out of his mind."

"Does the criticism trouble you?" Mary asked.

✷

"Not unless it bothers you," he answered. "My mind is made up, and my wife agrees. Your seminary is just what we need, an advanced school of high standards for young women at a moderate price."

Turning over more and more of the duties at Ipswich Seminary to Eunice and Abigail, Mary set to work at collecting the first contributions for the seminary, as yet unnamed and without a definite location.

Polly had returned from the South in early May, staying at Ipswich for a few weeks. At her doctor's advice, she took another leave from the seminary. This time she went west to Ohio, to Cincinnati to visit Catherine Beecher and to nearby Mt. Vernon to spend a week with a former pupil, Eliza Adams.

How Mary wished that Polly were well again! She still had dark circles under her eyes and was seldom able to walk without a cane. More than that, she lacked her usual cheery manner and often answered Mary sharply. "Perhaps this second leave will help her gain back her strength," Mary confided in Eunice.

It was through frequent correspondence that Mary kept Polly informed of the plans. When she wrote about the September meetings in her parlor at Ipswich, Polly answered, "Why not ask the ladies of the town to donate their charity money to the new seminary?"

And this Mary did. Sometimes she talked with the husbands, asking them to help too. She would even suggest that they "cut off one corner of their estates and give it to their wives to invest in a seminary for young ladies."

But more often she talked only to the woman of the household. "Just pretend you want a new shawl, a card table, or a new carpet and figure out how you might get it," she would say to a woman who seemed reluctant to give.

"She talked so fast," said a friend, "that her listeners never had a chance to put in a word." During these days it seemed that she was always in a hurry.

To her former pupils she wrote letters asking for any help they could give, from five cents to five hundred, and she even went to towns nearby and asked for donations. She was determined: she would raise a thousand dollars before leaving Ipswich.

She tried not to let the work at the seminary suffer, and she wouldn't overlook her own students either. There were recommendations to write for girls who wanted positions in the coming term, and there were applications that had to be answered, applications for teachers from the East and the West.

After considerable correspondence, she was able to locate the right teacher for a Dr. Charles Beatty in Steubenville, Ohio. He had written her as early as May of 1833. Then there were requests from Hamilton, Ohio, and from as far away as Monticello, Illinois.

"We need teachers desperately," wrote Miss Beecher. "We need an army of well-qualified teachers in the West. Send us all you can."

In July, 1834, Mary received an application for a teacher from Judge Wheaton of Norton, Massachusetts. "We would like you to furnish a teacher well acquainted with the system pursued at Ipswich and would like you to render what aid you can. . . ." the Judge had written.

※

In reply, Mary had suggested meeting the Judge in Boston, but a week later she was surprised to have his son appear at the door of the seminary.

"I have driven here from Norton in answer to your letter," Laban Wheaton, Jr., said soberly. "May I talk with you about our school?"

He told Mary that Norton was a small village some forty miles south of Boston near Taunton. Except for the Leonard Iron Works, the place, he explained, was largely agricultural, with about two thousand inhabitants. "The only schools are small grade schools. The nearest academy is in Taunton but that is for boys only, and the closest good seminary is in Uxbridge, a half day's journey away.

"Father wants a seminary for girls in Norton like yours here," young Wheaton said. And, staring off into space, he added quietly, "My sister Elizabeth died in March. It was a great shock to my father, and my wife and I think the school would be a much better memorial than all the monuments there are."

Mary glanced at this young man, slender and quite handsome. There was a strange quietness about him.

"Could you take charge of the school? We'll need teachers, but we'd like to offer you the principalship."

Mary said hastily, "But I'm not free to accept. It is true that I shall finish here in November, but I am already working on plans for my own seminary."

She watched him, folding and unfolding his hands nervously. "I'm sorry to hear of your loss," she said quietly. "I wish I might help you."

"Perhaps you can help us. Father has more than enough money, if you have any doubts. . . ."

"It's not a matter of money," Mary answered, "but I think I can help you. I have an assistant teacher who is very good. I feel sure I can work something out for you."

That evening Eunice listened intently to Mary's account of Laban Wheaton's visit. "I would like to recommend you for this position, Eunice."

"And what will you do, Mary?"

"I plan to go to Amherst as soon as Ipswich Seminary closes, but if you want me to, I'll come to Norton for a visit, or to help with the opening."

Eunice walked over to the window and looked out into the night. She wasn't sure. "I don't know the first thing about housing or the details of scheduling."

"I can help you, Eunice. I'll even take care of the housing arrangements if you want to arrange for the instruction and program."

Eunice settled herself again in the large armchair and sat for a while without speaking. The decision was a difficult one. She felt torn in her loyalties; and leaving Ipswich, her own family, and Miss Grant before the new seminary was ready hadn't been in her plans.

"I'll need some time to decide," she finally said.

Mary didn't try to urge her any further. Her patience paid off, for in a few days Eunice agreed to apply for the principalship. A few weeks later, Mary and Eunice took the stage to Norton to see the Wheatons and make final arrangements for the Norton Female Seminary that would open in the spring of 1835.

Together they worked on the prospectus, a statement of the aims and the courses, and by August of 1834 the ground across the road from the Wheaton homestead was broken

✱

for the two-story building, Seminary Hall, known today as the "Sem."

"This country is as flat as your hand," Mary told Orra Hitchcock. "But the students at Norton will have an open book for classes in botany. Woods and fields on every side!"

She tried not to compare Norton with the location in South Hadley that had been finally selected by the trustees as the site of her school. She recalled the committee's lengthy disputes about location and the final decisive meeting in Worcester on January 8, 1835. "It was below zero," she said, "but wrapped in buffalo robes, Mr. Hitchcock and I left Amherst a few hours before sunrise to attend the session. The choice was between South Deerfield and South Hadley. Ipswich, Andover, and Sunderland had already been voted down."

As Mary looked up at Mount Holyoke and across the rolling countryside, she was grateful that the decision brought her back to the Connecticut Valley. And she was especially grateful to the Hitchcocks, who welcomed her to Amherst, where Edward was now a full Professor of Geology and Natural History at the College.

In keeping with her promise to the Committee of Seven, Mary had collected over a thousand dollars before leaving Ipswich. She always referred to this collection from the ladies of Ipswich as "the cornerstone of her seminary."

In the 1830's in America, there were one hundred and twenty-six colleges for men and not a single one for women. Mary's seminary would be in actuality a college for young women sixteen years of age and older.

Until the South Hadley seminary opened its doors, Rev.

Roswell Hawks and Mary would travel many hundreds of miles together.

It wasn't until late in June that Mary saw her own family in Ashfield and by then Norton Female Seminary, later incorporated as Wheaton Female Seminary (March, 1837), had enrolled its first pupils.

"I wish you could have been there," Mary said, placing a small hassock at Freelove's feet. She looked up at her sister's face and thought she was paler than she had been in New York. She'll probably gain as soon as the warm weather comes, Mary thought.

"What did you say, Mary?" shouted Mr. Taylor. For several years Mr. Taylor had been quite deaf, and yet each time Mary visited, she forgot his affliction.

Drawing the chair closer, she said distinctly, "I was telling Freelove and Mother about the opening day at Miss Caldwell's school in Norton."

"Oh, were there many girls?" he asked.

"Fifty, all told," she answered, handing a copy of the prospectus to him. "That gives the names of the teachers and the schedule. I thought you and Mother might be interested."

Mary nodded at Freelove and smiled. "You should have seen some of the fancy shawls and bonnets. One young lady from Lancaster came all the way with a coachman. Such a flurry!" She chuckled softly.

"As far away as Lancaster?" said Freelove, a tone of surprise in her voice.

Mary nodded. "And even from Nantucket Island. It was a surprise to Miss Caldwell, since Norton is quite a bit off

✷

the regular coach route and about six miles from Taunton, the nearest inn. But the girls came—even the dull, gray day failed to dampen their spirits."

"And how do the plans for your school progress?" Freelove asked eagerly. "What have you decided to call it?"

Mary looked across at her sister, puzzled. She wondered how much the family knew about the criticism in the Boston papers. Her seminary was being labeled a "manual labor school" and the name that Edward Hitchcock had proposed, the Pangynaskean Seminary, called forth unexpected ridicule.

At the time she had been pleased with the novelty of the word. "Pure Greek," he said, "classical and appropriate. It means all the powers of woman—physical, intellectual, and moral." But editors, unfriendly to the school, tried to make it appear ridiculous.

"The trustees decided at their last meeting in April to call it simply Mount Holyoke Female Seminary," she said casually.

17

TROUBLED TIMES

Mary was glad to find Mr. White at home when she called the next morning. "I can never thank him enough for all he has done for me," she thought as she walked down the hill from her mother's home, "and here I am, still depending on his sound judgment—and Hannah's, too."

Seven children had been born and brought up in the White homestead that Mr. White had built in 1795, four boys and three girls. And she, too, had once called it "home." The boys had all gone to college and were doing well.

Only one girl, Amanda, had married. Mary wished she had seen Amanda the summer a few years before when she had come back with her two boys to visit. Why she had called on Mrs. Taylor, Mary didn't know and Amanda hadn't written. "She hoped to see you, I'm sure," said Freelove afterward, but Mary wasn't so sure.

✻

At the corner of the homestead, Mary pushed back the brass bellknob and was almost immediately greeted by Mr. White. "Mary Lyon, how good to see you! Come in. Come right in," he said cheerily.

As he started to lead her into the front room, she hesitated and said, "I've come on business . . . too."

"In that case," he turned and smiled at her, "let's go into my study and feel more at home."

She followed him into the well-loved room at the end of the hallway. "Mrs. White has gone over to the Paines', but Hannah will be right back. She's gone to the store." He pulled a chair up to his desk. "Sit here," he said, "and tell me how things are going with you."

"Accounts and records," she grimaced. "Would you look them over for me and tell me what I should do? I think I should have had a course in bookkeeping."

Hannah found the two of them there a half hour later when she returned. They were hunched over papers on a table they had drawn up in front of the fireplace.

"When you've finished, come out into the kitchen, Mary," she said. "And would you stay and have dinner with us?"

"Thank you, Hannah. I'd like to very much, but I must leave in time to get the three o'clock coach at South Deerfield for Amherst."

Mr. White promised to drive the two of them over to South Deerfield after dinner, giving them plenty of time to visit. "Or gossip," he said as he hurried out the side door.

In the kitchen, Mary and Hannah talked of the family, and finally of Amanda. Hannah had gone to Mackinac the summer of 1830 and had seen for herself the struggle and hardships of life in the backwoods. "She had me bring back the silk dresses she had taken," Hannah told Mary. "She had no need for them out there."

They talked a bit of Mary Stuart, who had come east from Mackinac to study, first at Buckland and then for three years at Ipswich. "She has a fiery spirit," said Mary, "but she earned her diploma."

Robert Stuart, an agent of the American Fur Company, who had helped organize a fur trading post in Astoria for John Jacob Astor, had made himself rich in the business and insisted that his children go east to school.

"And I have more news for you," said Hannah hastily. "The Ferrys have left Mackinac. They left in June for Grand Rapids, Michigan."

"Why?"

"Well, William has been poorly," Hannah explained, "and Amanda writes that they like the change so much, they'll not go back to the mission."

"Not ever preach again?" Mary asked doubtfully. It was hard to believe. She remembered how orthodox William had been and how firm in his belief—when she had been uncertain.

"That's right. He has already started in the lumber business."

Mary leaned back, amazed. She couldn't believe that the young minister she once knew had turned businessman.

Mary wouldn't live to know that after his death William would be noted not for his missionary work, but for his contribution to the industrial life of the West. In 1850 he laid out the town of Grand Haven on the shore of Lake Michigan and when he died seventeen years later, he left his family a legacy of a quarter of a million dollars.

※

"Perhaps he'll take a parish when he's well again," Mary said casually, half suspecting she had misunderstood Hannah.

"Perhaps," said Hannah.

But Mary and Hannah spent most of their time together talking about the plans for the new seminary at South Hadley.

Mary had no need to tell Hannah about the criticisms that had appeared in the press. She knew.

"I can't understand, though," Hannah remarked, "why Professor Andrews insists that you are proposing a 'manual labor' school."

"I haven't the least faith in a labor school, the kind where girls support themselves by such work as raising silk, spinning, or sewing, and that's probably what he has in mind."

"Why not answer his article, Mary?"

Mary shook her head. "I'd rather not start a newspaper feud," she confessed. "I really don't think it would help."

She recalled with some embarrassment that even the *Boston Recorder* had been unwilling to give free space in its columns for a series of articles on the seminary.

Picking up the April issue of the *Religious Magazine and Family Miscellany*, Hannah said, "Look at this! A Protestant nunnery indeed! I see nothing wrong with girls taking care of their own rooms and getting meals and cleaning up."

"It might make housekeeping even more respectable," Mary laughed at Hannah's concern.

"And it would be a great blessing in this 'flirting and primping' age," added Hannah.

There had been other criticisms. Charges of "unchristian" and "servile labor" had appeared in the press. The last November issue of the *Knickerbocker* had contained a long article by Catherine Sedgwick. "I had no idea she felt so strongly opposed to a boarding school," Mary remarked.

Active in the work of the new liberal church, Miss Sedgwick was the most popular authoress of the day, and Mary enjoyed her novels, and thought *The Travelers,* a book for young readers, especially good.

"Apparently she'd prefer to have girls educated at home," Hannah said, "but that day is fast disappearing."

"We can be thankful, though, for *Godey's Lady's Book,* and for women like Sarah Hale," said Mary. In every issue of this popular magazine, the best known of all American periodicals for women, its editor, Sarah J. Hale, urged favorable reform and better education for women. Mary's allies might be few, but Sarah Hale was one of them.

Even Polly didn't approve of having seminary girls do the domestic work of the school. Mary felt saddened when she began to realize that Polly no longer shared her views.

Mary would have to expect criticism, but she found it hard to accept Polly's opposition. Even so, she was determined to move ahead. She said to Edward Hitchcock, "The work is all important. No matter what is said, we must go on with it."

Her activities were staggering. Many wondered how she could do so much. She traveled by carriage in summer and by sleigh in winter from the Connecticut Valley to Boston and back, from Amherst to Norton and Abington, and once as far away as Falmouth on Cape Cod. Her notebooks listed as contributors over eight hundred persons in some ninety towns and villages all over New England. "They turned out their pockets," she reported, "to give the first $27,000."

A farmer in Townsend, Massachusetts, gave six cents.

"That's all I have," he said, "but it's yours if it'll do any good."

"It will," she said gratefully. She thought back to her farm days and the mountain home. She'd show the farmer and all other contributors that their money was well invested.

On February 11, 1836, the first milestone was reached. Both houses of the Massachusetts legislature authorized the trustees of Mount Holyoke Female Seminary to hold "real and personal estate" not exceeding in value a hundred thousand dollars and devoted exclusively to the purposes of education. On March 2, Mary heard the five trustees accept the act, and knew the seminary had become a reality. A building committee was soon appointed.

But it took a much longer time to decide on the actual site in South Hadley—so long that even Mary grew nervous, fearful that continued delay might mean the end of her plans. Finally, five months later, on July 31, the trustees selected the location, across the Holyoke range south of Amherst, and on October 3, Mary watched as the cornerstone was laid.

A week later she wrote Eunice, "The stones, and brick, and mortar speak a language which vibrates through my very soul. How much thought and how much feeling have I had on this general subject in years that are past. And I have indeed lived to see the time when a body of gentlemen have ventured to lay the cornerstone of an edifice which will cost about fifteen thousand dollars, and will be an institution for the education of women—surely, the Lord hath remembered our low estate. . . ."

As soon as the building got under way, Mary went to

board with the Condits, who lived just north of the seminary site.

She worked late and long, checking and listing, writing for help with the furniture, and looking after details of cupboards, closets, shelves, and latches.

Scarcely a morning passed that she didn't join Mr. Andrew Porter, a member of the Building Committee, who had finally left his own business to give full time to supervising the construction of Seminary Hall. She was both eager and inquisitive.

One morning soon after the first rows of bricks had been put in place to form the basement walls, she started across the road for her usual tour. She was surprised to see Mr. Porter hurrying toward her, waving his arms and pointing to the building.

"What's happened?" she called loudly, rushing to meet him.

"The wall has collapsed!" Her heart sank. She looked at the discouragement on Mr. Porter's face and asked, "Was anyone hurt?"

"No one, thank the good Lord. The workmen were all at breakfast."

"Then we'll start all over again," Mary said.

By the late spring of 1837 the walls of the four-story brick building were in place. To Mary it had five floors, for the basement, containing a dining hall, six small rooms, and a large domestic hall with washtubs, stoves, and lamps was to run the length of the building. Here the girls would not only wash their own clothes but boil, wash, and rinse the laundry for the seminary. For this work, Mary wanted the most efficient arrangement.

✳

She wrote to Polly, as she thought what had to be done before the seminary opened in November, "It seems like looking down a precipice of many hundred feet, which I must descend. I can only avoid looking at the bottom, and fix my eye on the nearest stone, till I have safely reached it."

But the "stones" were many. Besides securing her teachers and making decisions on the applications of students, Mary was faced with the almost hopeless struggle of getting furniture and furnishings for the rooms. Her urgent letters brought a donation of more than $230 from Eunice Caldwell and the Wheaton girls to furnish a parlor, and a gift of $269 from teachers and pupils at Ipswich.

But she had thirty bedrooms and three parlors to furnish, as well as the dining room and kitchen and the classrooms. Carefully she composed a circular letter and sent copies to all the women she knew might help. "Can you get your town or a group of women there to furnish a room?" she pleaded. "One room will cost about sixty dollars."

Gradually donations and contributions came in. One lady promised to supply almost all the crockery, and furniture for about a dozen rooms was pledged. Still there wasn't nearly enough, and promised pledges were suddenly not coming in fast enough.

Thirty students had already been accepted and in a few months the seminary building should be ready. She would have to make another appeal. She did.

She sent out a second circular letter, this time to the young ladies who had been accepted. "Could you bring with you some or all of the following articles, two pair of sheets and pillow cases, two towels, two blankets, a comforter, a bed quilt, an underbed tick and a pair of pillows, and two

TROUBLED TIMES

silver teaspoons or one tablespoon. Plan to mark your things well so they may be returned to you when you leave." Her appeal closed with, "I need to know before you come what you can bring. The number of scholars I can receive may depend on your reply."

Replies were more promising than Mary had anticipated. She could definitely plan to open in November. She would tell the trustees of her decision at the October meeting. Within a week she would be ready to move into her rooms in Seminary Hall.

"Why not postpone the opening until next spring?" Mr. Tyler proposed.

"But why, gentlemen?"

"It's just that business is in a bad way right now, and pledges that should be redeemed are not coming in. The financial situation might ease up by spring."

"But the building is ready," Mary pleaded.

She turned to Mr. Hawks for support, but he laid an empty purse on the table, saying, "It's all I have to show for my weeks of effort." Mr. Hawks had just returned from a long trip soliciting funds. "I suggest we postpone the opening day."

But Mary remained adamant. "Won't we have enough money to last a year without the redeemed pledges?" she asked, looking around the table at the serious faces.

The answer was affirmative. That was all she needed to know.

Mary realized that there was economic panic and unrest. The papers were full of stories of debts and losses. Business had been hard hit. Money was frightfully scarce, she understood, especially in cities, where prices of food and clothing

*

had gone up as much as a hundred per cent. Some blamed President Jackson for the four years of what was called "runaway land jobbing." Others said it was the decline of the China trade.

But whatever caused the national panic of 1837, Mary couldn't be persuaded to put off the opening date. "I'll welcome the first class of Mount Holyoke Female Seminary on November 8," she told the Board. And she left the room, walking briskly out the door and across the grounds, the pink ribbons on her lace cap flying, a look of grim determination on her face.

18

HAPPY DAYS

"Can you come two weeks early and help me?" Mary wrote Nancy Everett of Wrentham, Massachusetts. "You are one of the few girls I have asked to offer their services before the seminary opens."

Mary couldn't have asked students who would be more helpful. They put on long aprons over their silk and gingham dresses and washed floors, cleaned windows, and helped sew blankets and comforters. They did everything that either Miss Lyon or Abigail Moore asked, and did it with a willingness that warmed Mary's heart. "Their enthusiasm is catching," she told Abigail.

Mary's niece had become her aunt's "right hand." She had resigned from her position in Virginia to help at South Hadley and, if possible, to study part time.

"I'm calling you the family superintendent," Mary told Abigail, "and Mrs. Hawks will help you with the girls. She

✳

is boarding them in her home in Belchertown until we are ready to open the dining room."

It was a busy two weeks. The building swarmed with "helpers." Mr. and Mrs. Daniel Safford had arrived from Boston and Mr. Andrew Porter came over from nearby Monson every day to oversee the carpenters and painters.

"I want the bedroom floors painted a plain color," Mary had told Mr. Porter. "Yellow will make the rooms look brighter on dark days." Each room would have a Franklin stove, and if the girls wished to furnish a small rug they might use one in front of the stove. A bed, a dresser, and a desk and chair would be enough furniture for each girl. "Comfortable but simple and neat," Mary explained.

Yet with all the work and careful preparations, Mary had to admit that even more needed to be done. The rooms were not quite ready, the carpet had not been laid in the front hallway, and, worst of all, there were no front steps. Mr. Porter had the grounds to clear, for deep beds of sand were still piled high around the foundation.

"We'll make do with what we have," Mary told her teachers who had arrived early the day before. She had been especially pleased to see Eunice, who had left Wheaton Seminary to become her associate principal and had brought with her a Wheaton teacher, Mary Smith.

"It's so good to see you, Eunice, and to have you open the seminary with me," Mary said later that evening as they planned the schedule. "I'll take charge of the housekeeping, but I'll want your help with the instructional program. I expect we'll have about fifty girls."

But over seventy girls arrived the opening day, from

Brattleboro, Vermont, to Hartford, Connecticut, and from Ohio and Pennsylvania. No one seemed to mind that Mr. Porter was still tacking down the carpet in the hallway, or that the entrance was through a side door that led onto a porch and into a small parlor.

Girls came by stage and private carriages and open buggies most of the day, November 8, 1837. Mary, in her green silk dress and small white turban, tried to be on hand to greet each new girl. Her cheer and vivacity gave no indication that she had risen before sunup to bake ten loaves of bread and three pans of gingerbread.

Stage after stage brought happy loads of girls, and the teachers and assistants enjoyed with them their delight and "raptures" over the sight of Mount Tom and the Connecticut River from the third- and fourth-floor windows.

Some of the boys from Amherst College milled around, helping to carry trunks and valises upstairs and generally enjoying the excitement. One young man carried a large trunk up the stairs to the second floor and then proceeded to search through the bedrooms.

"Are you lost?" Miss Caldwell called to him from the landing.

"Oh, no," he said, somewhat startled. "I . . . I was looking for someone." And before Eunice could ask another question, he had bounded up the stairs to the third floor.

He looked into the nearest room and then stood for a while, waiting. There she was! He had helped her carry up an armload of books the day before and all he knew was her first name. She and her roommate were too busy trying to put a bed together to hear him enter.

※

They nearly dropped the sides of the bed when they saw him standing nearby. "May I help you, Miss Nancy?" he said, taking hold of the headboard.

"Why, Mr. Dwight, how did you know I was up here?"

"I looked around," he said, smiling. "And how did you know my name?"

"A friend told me," she said. They laughed and Nancy said, "This is my roommate, Marian Hawks—and I'm Nancy Everett. We'd be most appreciative."

John Dwight corded the bed for them and stayed long enough to ask Nancy if he could call Friday evening. She hesitated, but agreed. And eighteen-year-old Nancy Everett fell in love. It was the first love story of the new "college." Four years later Mary would attend the wedding in the Congregational Church just north of the seminary grounds, and Nancy and John Dwight would settle in South Hadley.

For Mary, November 8 was the realization of years of dreams and planning. At four o'clock Mary rang the schoolroom bell and called together all the students and teachers. With prayers by South Hadley's minister, Rev. Joseph D. Condit, and a short address by Rev. Joel Hawes, a visiting minister from Boston and later a trustee, Mount Holyoke Female Seminary was in session.

Examinations would be taken on the following day by all the girls to place them in their right courses. In setting up the program, Mary had followed rather closely that of the men's colleges. She had omitted any study of ancient or modern languages, and had added more than the usual amount of science and mathematics. "My teachers will be prepared well," she told Eunice. "A solid, extensive, and well-balanced English education of three years . . . preparing them to be educators of children and youth. . . . It's the kind of schooling I should have chosen for myself if I could have planned my education."

Remembering well her own early limitations and interests, Mary saw to it that the girls had several hours a week of instruction in vocal music and linear and perspective drawing, and piano lessons were offered at an additional fee to those who wished them.

Besides the lessons and classes, each girl gave two hours a day to some domestic work. "But it is not part of your educational program," Mary explained to them. "You do not come to be taught domestic work, but you need to make things easier for the seminary and to keep down the tuition."

"It's my week to set the tables," one of the students wrote home. "If you can imagine it, I placed and lighted two fires in the kitchen stoves, cut ten loaves of bread, and put on many pitchers of water."

The days were fully scheduled, from the rising bell at six in the morning to the retiring bell at a quarter of nine. And when washing day arrived on Tuesday, every girl turned out to help, boiling and rinsing, wringing and hanging. "We divided them into five circles," explained Abigail when she wrote her mother, "and three out of each circle are chosen to hang the clothes in the large court at the rear of the building."

"A schedule helps to make good students," Mary explained when a girl complained that she had no free time. "In that way we shall not waste time." And every day at four o'clock the girls gave accounts of the day to their

✱

teachers, reporting absences, tardiness, talking without permission, breaking silent study hours, and, as one student said later, "a thousand other things."

But life at Mount Holyoke Seminary had its lighter moments. Mary allowed Amherst boys to call and meet the girls in the downstairs parlors. And there were sleigh rides, song fests, and molasses candy pulls in the winter, and in the spring and summer sessions groups went berrying in big hay wagons, carrying tin pails and willow baskets.

Once in a great while there was a picnic on Mount Holyoke. Mary always remembered one in particular. It had been an unusually warm spring day. "We've had such a cold spring," Mary announced at breakfast, "I declare a holiday for everyone today."

Lunches packed, the girls piled into wagons that Mary had rented and, with careful directions to the teachers and the drivers, she waved them on their way.

But scarcely two hours had passed before she had word that a young man from Amherst had been seen riding posthaste through the notch toward the College. Whatever should she do? She knew only too well that the college boys would soon be flocking to the mountain.

Sending for Mr. Hawks, she asked him to go at once to bring the girls back. The holiday ended unhappily—and early.

"It seems," complained one of the girls as they were climbing down the mountainside, "that we escaped the Lyon's den only to fall into the Hawks' nest." That story soon made the rounds of the seminary, and Mary chuckled to herself whenever she heard it.

Eager to have a seminary of high standards, Mary kept

to the regulations and every Saturday afternoon held a "family meeting." "She talks to us frankly about everything," Lucy wrote her mother in Stockton. "Even about our speech and behavior when we go out."

Mary preached, advised, and counseled as though the girls were her own daughters. She explained the Commandments and discussed openly the meaning to them of the Seventh. "Keep away from yourself all unchaste thoughts, words, and actions," she always repeated from the *Shorter Catechism*.

"And don't be in a hurry to get married," she would tell the sixteen- and seventeen-year-old girls. "Wait until you have finished your education. Then you'll be better wives and mothers."

"I wonder what the girls say about me when I preach to them about not getting married too young," Mary said to Orra one day while visiting with the Hitchcocks in Amherst.

"Probably just what my girls say to me when I preach or try to advise them," Orra answered quickly. She looked up and smiled, "Catherine thinks I'm a bit old-fashioned."

"That reminds me. I haven't heard from your girls in a long time. How is Catherine, and what is my namesake Mary doing with herself?"

"The girls are fine, and Mary writes that she still likes her studies at Ipswich Seminary. She always writes that she misses you."

Mary frowned slightly. "I'd like to go back to Ipswich soon and visit the girls, and I'd enjoy seeing Eunice and Polly again, but somehow I never have time." She sighed and for a moment hesitated. Then she added, "The last time I went was three years ago—to Polly's wedding."

✷

"I remember," said Orra. "You were quite concerned."

After a short silence Mary said, "I could never quite understand why Polly wanted to get married at her age. Besides, she had been ill a long time, and I thought she was quite content living with Mrs. Briggs in Dedham. Polly is older than I am."

"But forty is not too old, Mary. You know, I was beginning to think you were planning to marry. What is this I hear about Mr. Lamb?"

"What do you mean?" Mary asked. "He has called on me a few times. Is that it?" She tried to appear casual.

"That's what I mean, Mary."

"You're teasing me," Mary laughed lightly.

"No, I'm not. He's a good man, even though he is a widower with six young daughters. With all your experience with girls, you could manage."

"I shall confess, Orra, but just to you. I'd rather you didn't tell Edward. He proposed to me a week ago, and I refused him. If I married, I would have to give up my work at the seminary."

That was all that was said, and Orra knew better than to ask any more questions. Mary never mentioned Mr. Lamb again.

On her way back to South Hadley the next day, Mary was keenly aware of the beauty of the foliage and was reminded of another beautiful trip two years earlier when she rode up to Ashfield to her sister Freelove's wedding. She had gone to the wedding with mixed feelings. Her sister was marrying Elisha Wing, widower of her older sister Jemima, who had died just the year before. Jemima had left seven children, the oldest sixteen and the baby two and a half.

"I'll bring up Jemima's children," Freelove had told Mary with a contentment that Mary hadn't seen in Freelove since her return from the West.

But grief quickly followed happiness, and in September her mother sent word for Mary to come at once.

"It'll be a hard birth, I suspect," the doctor explained to Mary. "I had to put her to bed to keep down the swelling in her ankles. See that she doesn't get upset or do too much."

"I'll take good care of her," Mary promised.

But the birth was more difficult than even the doctor had expected, and at that time in the nineteenth century there was nothing more Mary or anyone else could do to help. The tiny baby son died in Mary's arms as she sat near the bedside, and three days later she watched Freelove quietly slip away. For the first time in years Mary gave in to her grief, sobbing as she had when Aaron left the mountain home.

Within the year both her mother and stepfather died. "Can you think how lonely it was . . . with no brother or sister by my side," she wrote Aaron. "But a few years ago, and we seemed an unbroken circle."

Mary thought back over the years to a day in 1810 when she rode up the mountainside, feeling deserted and alone. But she felt no more bitterness. She had her seminary home, and there were her nieces and nephews to help.

From the very beginnings of the seminary, Mary had offered her nieces free tuition, and several came to study and some prepared to teach. Mary was proud of the girls, and it pleased her most when Abigail Moore and Lucy Lyon stayed to teach in her school.

She did all she could, too, to encourage her nephews to

※

get a college education, sometimes helping financially. Stukely, Rosina's boy, went to Yale College in New Haven, Connecticut, and Mason Moore, to nearby Amherst College. The boys often visited Aunt Mary.

"I spent part of a spring vacation with her," Stukely recalled, "and when I was ready to leave, she slipped a five-dollar bill into my hand."

"Take this to help out on college expenses. I know you have many."

"I'll preach my first sermon for you, Aunt Mary," he had promised.

"Just be a good minister," she said, smiling at the handsome lad.

Daughters of her friends also came to Mount Holyoke, including Catherine and Mary Hitchcock. There were ministers' daughters, too, for Mary offered a specially low tuition to them. Finally, Amanda's daughter arrived from Michigan, and her mother wrote to thank Mary for accepting her.

A quiet, thoughtful girl of nineteen, Amanda Harwood Ferry was as pretty as her mother, with dark curly hair and dark eyes. But she had her father's dimpled chin and, as Mary soon discovered, a mind of her own.

Although young Amanda seldom had to report herself for failure to obey the many rules of the school, she often seemed indifferent.

"Are you all right?" Mary asked one evening, going to her room to talk with her.

"Yes, Aunt Mary, why?"

"And are you content here?" Mary continued.

"Well, I guess so," she said, "but I really miss my friends and the family in Grand Rapids. It's very different here."

She went on to explain that she had never been to an all-girls' school before, that she found it hard to stay in and be supervised.

Silent for a while, Amanda looked over at her aunt and confessed, "I want to marry Mr. Hall and live in Michigan. I hope it doesn't offend you, Aunt Mary, but I don't want to teach school when I get back. I have already written Mother."

Young Amanda left in July, at the end of the term. Mary doubted that she would see either daughter or mother again.

19

A TENTH ANNIVERSARY

When Mary opened the seminary in November of 1837 her "experiment" in higher education for women was questioned and doubted by many. But in ten years its influence was felt throughout the nation and in every quarter of the globe.

The year after the seminary opened, Eunice left to be married and for the next five years Mary worked alone as head of the seminary. No one would ever know how hard these years were. But she cleared the debt that resulted from unpaid pledges, kept intact the domestic feature of the seminary, and maintained high standards.

In 1842, Mary appointed two of her teachers as co-principals. "I need you to talk for me," she told Abigail on her way to a Board meeting. "I am so deaf now."

She had not only grown somewhat deaf but her auburn hair had long streaks of gray in it, and she seemed a bit shorter and heavier. Her walk was no less brisk, however, and she hurried from one task to another without relaxing.

"God will hold you accountable for loitering," she would say to any students who tarried in the hallway or on the stairs.

As the demands for missionaries and for missionary work increased in America, Mary labored with even greater zeal for the cause. She permitted prayer meetings to be held once a month in the seminary hall, and was gratified when one of her first graduates, Fidelia Fisk, accepted a foreign mission. In the years that followed, Mary would see more than thirty students go into missionary work, some out west in Michigan, California, and Oregon, some abroad.

When Abigail and Lucy both married and left in 1846, Mary wrote Polly, "I feel the loss of my two nieces very much. Abigail has left for India, and now Lucy sails next month from New York for China."

But Mary put aside her personal grief and personal loss. "The work of the Lord must go forward," she told Orra Hitchcock one day, "and the religious life of the seminary." Mary was well aware of the occasional criticisms of a course of study that was heavily intellectual.

"No one need fear that Mount Holyoke is all literary and scientific," Orra said. "You can be sure of that."

"As much of a scientist as Mary is," Orra told her husband that evening, "she is a devoted Christian." Mr. Hitchcock, appointed President of Amherst College on Mr. Humphrey's retirement in 1845, was serving as a trustee of the seminary.

"Yes," he agreed. "She may not hold with the literal meaning of the Bible any more than I do, but she believes strongly in prayer and faith."

*

Mary told the girls that archaeologists were contantly discovering new things that referred to the Bible. She didn't sympathize with the ideas of Hell and damnation, and in that sense, she knew, she was not a true Puritan.

Her faith, however, prevented her from accepting the growing custom of festivities at Christmas. Thanksgiving was the outstanding holiday of the year at Mount Holyoke, as it was throughout New England, but Mary refused to observe Christmas except as a day of worship—and work. The regular work of the seminary would continue, on washday or composition day or any day of the week, except for a few hours set aside for meditation.

As soon as the spring term opened in 1847, Mary began to plan for Anniversary Week. She thought back over the past ten years. It hardly seemed possible that she would hold her tenth graduation in August and that the seventh class would receive diplomas for completing the three-year course.

She sent out invitations to friends and former students. She selected carefully the student compositions that would be read aloud on graduation morning, Thursday, August 5. Rev. Herman Humphrey, former President of Amherst College, would be the speaker and Mr. Condit would hand out the diplomas. She couldn't have been more pleased— or ready.

She rose early Wednesday morning to be on hand to help Miss Whitman, her associate principal, receive the guests. There had already been two days of public examinations for the girls, the usual procedure in the 1840's, and more than the usual number of visitors had attended them. She imag-

A TENTH ANNIVERSARY

ined that the dinner following the exercises would bring even more guests.

As Mary finished dressing, she smoothed down the folds of her lavender silk gown and went over to the bureau. Looking through the pile of caps in the top drawer, she took out a lace one with narrow green ribbons. Then she found a pair of short black gloves, also made of lace and bound in braid. "My," she thought, "I have become a trifle vain." And then added, "It's all for my girls. A gingham dress would never do on this important occasion."

Mary, who as a girl had worn homespun and had cared less about her appearance than about her studies, now dressed with care. In the winter she wore dark-green or wood-color delaine, but in the summer she preferred gingham or French calico frocks, usually brown or blue with small figures. She usually wore something white around her neck and carried a linen pocket handkerchief.

And there was the green velvet bag with her shawls and neckpieces. She had a newer bag, a black one for her handkerchief and keys, but she loved the old green one. She supposed by now everyone knew that. "I'll carry the black one," she said to herself. She placed the worn green bag carefully in the drawer. She would seldom use it again. Then she went over to the table to check the acceptances.

It was as though she were actually checking non-acceptances. She kept thinking of those who couldn't come. Neither Polly nor Eunice could accept, and the Wheatons of Norton and the Whites in Ashfield had sent their regrets.

And she thought of those who were away. It would be the first anniversary without her nieces Abigail and Lucy.

✻

By the time the examinations were finished on Tuesday afternoon, nearly all the expected guests had arrived. There was real excitement about the homecoming for the "daughters" of Mount Holyoke. "It looks like an opening day," Mary told Miss Whitman. "We haven't had so much hustle and bustle since our girls arrived last November to register."

Dormitory rooms were filled by Wednesday noon. All the girls who were not graduating had left, and their rooms were being used for alumnae and guests. "If others come," Miss Whitman said, "they'll have to make other arrangements."

"There's the inn," said Mary, "or a friend's, possibly."

But several more guests came and Mary didn't have the heart to turn them away. "We'll find a place somewhere," she said. "Ask some of the girls to use the parlors on the second floor. They are carpeted and the girls can spread blankets on the floor."

Miss Whitman waited a moment. She was a tall woman, gentle and calm, who didn't always understand Mary, but neither did she oppose her. They had worked well as principal and co-principal, and Mary had gained some relief from her heavy duties.

Besides, Mary had been able with Miss Whitman's help to secure a superintendent for the domestic service. Mary hadn't baked a loaf of bread or helped in the kitchen for a long time.

"Are you sure this is the last guest, Miss Lyon?" Miss Whitman asked.

"Yes, quite sure," Mary nodded as she went back to her room. It would be a while before supper and she had the diplomas to sign.

A TENTH ANNIVERSARY

It seemed only a matter of minutes when Miss Whitman was back. Mary looked up from her writing to find her standing at her elbow. Miss Whitman had learned that she had to stand close to Mary unless she wanted to repeat herself at least once.

"We have another visitor," she said, frowning. "I don't like to bother you, but she is insistent."

"But the rooms are filled. We haven't another bed," Mary said sharply. She lifted her eyebrows and added, "or floor."

"I know," quickly answered Miss Whitman. "I know and I told her so, but she insists on seeing you." Miss Whitman waited patiently for Mary to put aside the diplomas.

"What are we going to do?" she asked.

"I guess I'll have to see her. What did you say her name was?"

"I don't know. I didn't like to ask too many questions." Miss Whitman paused. "She looks so pathetic—must have traveled all night by coach. She finally said she had a daughter here last year."

"Take her to the parlor, Miss Whitman," Mary said, a tone of impatience in her voice. "Tell her I'll be right there."

Mary brushed back the hair from her forehead. The August day had been unusually warm and Mary had removed her lace cap. She put on a fresh one, smoothed the folds of her skirt, and hurried along the corridor.

Opening the door, she saw a small, slightly built woman looking out the window. She was dressed in a plain brown cotton and wore a large brimmed bonnet.

"You wanted to see me, Miss Whitman said," Mary started across the room and then hesitated.

The stranger turned. "I came to see if you had a room

177

for me in the seminary," she said, pushing the bonnet away from her face.

"But there is no room left. What about the Inn? It is not far from here and . . ."

"I have just come from there," the stranger interrupted, "and they sent me to you. Perhaps I should have gone right on to Ashfield after all." She reached down and picked up a small valise that she had placed near the window.

Suddenly Mary remembered a dark-haired girl in a red silk dress with lace and ruffles, and her eyes filled with tears.

Then the stranger walked toward Mary with her hand outstretched. "I don't think you know me, Mary Lyon."

From a past of more than twenty years came a manner and a tone of voice that Mary had loved so dearly. "Oh, yes, I do know you, Amanda. I do know you!"

Mary clasped her closely, as she had when they were young together in Ashfield, and tears streamed down Amanda's face. Was this the Amanda she had known so well—the Amanda who had studied with her, was a "sister" to her in the early days at Sanderson Academy, and had chided her often for inkspots on her dresses and for soiled collars?

"There is room! There is room!" Mary reassured her. "You can stay with me in my room."

Amanda White Ferry stayed on at the seminary with Mary until the following Monday, when she left to spend a few days with her family in Ashfield.

In the years that followed, Amanda would be glad that she had finally had the courage and love to return to Mary's tenth anniversary. Both her father and mother, Mr. and Mrs. White, died a year later, and for Mary there would be only one more Anniversary Week.

20

A CHAIN OF IVY

In spite of the increase in applications and registration each year, Mary tried to greet all her girls by name. She found it more difficult in the fall of 1847, with the school doubled in attendance to over two hundred students. But she still made every effort to know the girls and to recognize their problems and their differences.

The day before Christmas, Mary had held the traditional meeting asking the girls to keep Christ's birthday a holy one and to devote several hours to silent meditation. At the close of the meeting it was customary for the girls to stand up in answer to the question, "How many are willing to do this?" Looking down from the platform, Mary saw two "new" students still in their seats, their hands tightly folded in their laps. She waited a while, but they didn't stand up.

"Please sit down—all of you," she said with as much calmness as she could muster.

✻

She thought, I haven't made myself clear. That's it.

"I repeated most of my talk," she explained later to Miss Whitman, "but I changed the question. I asked all those to stand who were not willing."

"I couldn't believe it," she went on. "Emily stood up alone, and remained standing while I dismissed all the rest."

Mary hesitated, recalling the slight tremor in Emily Dickinson's voice when she had reprimanded her.

Mary thought of the times in her own youth when she had felt equally defiant and wondered why she hadn't been able to see herself in this strong-willed girl, with hair as red as her own.

Emily later told her roommate, Emily Norcross, a cousin of hers from Monson, "I wanted to sit down with you, but once I had faced Miss Lyon, I felt I couldn't change my mind without a good reason—and I had none." Emily wished she were home in Amherst. Her father, a lawyer in town, and her brother Austin would understand.

So Emily Dickinson, recognized after her death as one of America's finest poets, packed her bags and took the stage home. Later, though, she wrote to a friend, "I love this seminary, and all the teachers are bound to my heart by ties of affection. . . . Miss Lyon and all the teachers seem to consult our comfort and happiness in everything they do."

Mary was pleased when Emily returned to finish the term and take her examinations with her class, the middle group. She still made every effort to encourage girls to stay for a full year and, when possible, to complete the three-year course for teaching.

But as the seminary increased in size, Mary found she

needed more rest and often went to visit the Porters in Monson, some twenty miles away. The demands on her time and energy were even further increased when she lost the help of Miss Whitman just after the seminary opened in November, 1848. Too sick to continue working, Miss Whitman was forced to take a leave of absence and Mary felt the added strain.

"I get chills at times," she told Mrs. Porter, "but it's probably just being tired." She didn't tell her friend that she occasionally stayed in bed all day with a bad headache and that at times she felt dizzy.

But there were days when Mary was well again and she soon forgot the dizziness and the headaches as she bustled about looking after a homesick girl, helping in the chemistry lab with an experiment, or checking supplies for the classrooms.

She would have gone to New York with her teachers during the January vacation, but she had promised to spend it with the Porters. "My teachers wanted me to sit for a portrait," she told them, "but I felt I would be better to have quiet and rest with you." Her teachers had urged her for some time to have a portrait painted. "To celebrate my years at South Hadley," she said. "I do appreciate their thoughtfulness, and perhaps I should have gone. They wanted to pay all my expenses, too."

Less than a month later, shortly after Mary had returned from Monson, an epidemic of influenza struck the seminary. Sick with a cold herself, Mary refused to go to bed, but went about nursing and comforting the girls.

When Sarah Wingate developed high fever and Dr.

✳︎

Brooks had to be called in, many of the girls became frightened and those who had not caught the flu or were feeling better wanted to go home.

"If any of you is really afraid," Mary said, "you may." She didn't try to urge them to stay, and she felt far too exhausted to "moralize."

She bowed her head and said simply, "I am not afraid, and I shall stay." She sat for long hours at the bedside of Sarah Wingate, placing cool compresses on her forehead. Sometimes Sarah's sister Ann, who had entered the seminary in the fall with Sarah, watched with Mary. But Sarah failed to throw off the fever. "I doubt that she will live more than the day," Dr. Brooks said at the last. "She has incurable erysipelas."

The sad message was sent to her parents in Weare, New Hampshire, and Sarah's father arrived just a few hours before her death.

During a brief service in the winter darkness at four in the morning, Mary collapsed and had to be carried to her room.

"Father and I went to her room afterwards to say goodbye," Ann wrote, "but Miss Lyon must have been having a chill. The bed shook under her."

The next day Mary recovered sufficiently to sit up, but the doctor persuaded her to remain as quiet as possible. She spent her fifty-second birthday in bed with high fever, and the same morning the mail brought news of the suicide of Elisha Wing, Jemima's oldest son.

"He was only twenty-two," she was heard to moan, "and not a converted Christian."

That evening Mary fell into a state of unconsciousness from which she never recovered. For nearly three days she talked unintelligibly day and night, without letup in a worried, high-strung manner. Dr. Brooks pronounced with certainty that Miss Lyon had congestion of the brain that accompanied malignant erysipelas.

A week later, March 5, 1849, Mary Mason Lyon died. Founder of the first college for women, she was buried on the seminary grounds, a little south of what was then an orchard, within view of the rooms on the south side of Seminary Hall. Telegraphic wire carried the sad news from city to city.

Daughter of a farmer from Putnam's Hill in western Massachusetts, she had put into practice her ideas of higher education for women and offered an inexpensive schooling for women like herself in the "common paths of life."

"It might be difficult to show exactly wherein her great skill and success lay," wrote her first biographer, her lifelong friend Edward Hitchcock.

Mary would have been pleased to know that fifty years later, in 1893, her seminary finally adopted the name of Mount Holyoke College. That same year the women of Massachusetts honored Mary's memory with a tablet at the Chicago World's Fair.

She would have been pleased, too, to know that, in the years that followed, her seminary was an inspiration to other educators. Through her teaching she had touched the lives of more than three thousand students, many of whom became teachers and pioneers like herself. By 1885 more than 150 Mount Holyoke graduates had labored in foreign lands, and seminaries like her school had spread to Turkey, South Africa, Spain, and Persia. Direct trace of her influence could also be seen in the United States in such schools as Oxford and Painesville, Ohio, and in Mills College, California.

The first principal of Vassar College, founded in 1861, Miss Hannah Lyman, had been one of her students at Ipswich Seminary, and the first principal of Wellesley College, founded in 1870, Miss Ada L. Howard, was a Mount Holyoke graduate and teacher.

Wheaton College in Norton, Massachusetts, owed its beginnings and much of its strength to Mary's generous assistance in the opening years when Eunice Caldwell was its first principal.

Today Mary Lyon would be amazed at the tremendous advances in the education of girls—the extensive opportunities for girls as well as boys to have free education through the twelfth grade, and the acceptance of women in colleges and universities, not only in private and public liberal arts colleges for women but also in large universities once open only to men, such as Harvard and Yale.

Today, too, she would be pleased and gratified to find that her ideas have "endured from generation to generation" as she had hoped, that the ideal of self-development for service is still central to the liberal arts education at Mount Holyoke College, and that since 1935 the College has strengthened its professional education of teachers by offering a Master of Arts in Teaching.

Many have been the honors and tributes paid to Mary Lyon over the years. And in 1905, recognized as an outstanding teacher and educator, she was chosen along with Emma Willard as one of the first women in America's Hall of Fame at New York University. A Mary Lyon Memorial Fund was established at Mount Holyoke in 1951 for the purchase of books on chemistry, her favorite subject. And each graduating class of the College pays tribute to her memory, placing a chain of ivy around her grave on the campus.

But her deeds and words were her finest epitaph. She had opened a door for women's higher education and had encouraged young women to honor teaching by improving their minds and hearts.

"Teach, as Christ taught, to do good," Mary Lyon told her students. "Dollars and cents can never pay the faithful minister, nor the faithful teacher." . . . And, recalling a tool she had often seen her brother use to cut hay on the farm, she would add, "Whoever has a willing heart may sharpen the sickle and help gather in the harvest."

SELECTED LIST OF AUTHORITIES

BY MARY LYON

[Lyon, Mary], *A Missionary Offering, or Christian Sympathy, Personal Responsibility; and the Present Crisis in Foreign Missions.* Boston: Crocker and Brewster, 1843.

ABOUT MARY LYON

Bailey, George H., *An Address on the One Hundredth Anniversary of Mary Lyon's Birth.* Buckland Public Library: unpub., 1897.

Bradford, Gamaliel, *Portraits of American Women.* Boston & New York: Houghton Mifflin Co., 1919.

Fisk, Fidelia, *Recollections of Mary Lyon.* Boston: American Tract Society, c1866.

Gilchrist, Beth Bradford, *The Life of Mary Lyon.* Boston & New York: Houghton Mifflin Co., 1910.

Goodsell, Willystine, Ed., *Pioneers of Women's Education in the United States: Emma Willard, Catherine Beecher, Mary Lyon.* New York: McGraw-Hill, 1931.

Hitchcock, Edward, Comp., *Power of Christian Benevolence Illustrated in the Life and Labors of Mary Lyon.* Northampton: Hopkins, Bridgman, and Co., 1852.

Howe, Mark A. D., *Classic Shades: Five Leaders of Learning and Their Colleges*. Boston: Little, Brown and Co., 1928.

Humphrey, Heman. *The Shining Path*. Northampton: J. & L. Metcalf, 1849.

Lansing, Marion, Ed., *Mary Lyon Through Her Letters*. Clinton, Mass.: Colonial Press Inc., 1937.

Mary Lyon: *The Christian Teacher*. New York: The Century Co., n.d.

Miller, Mary Esther G., *"Personal Recollections of Mary Lyon"* in *History and Proceedings*. Deerfield, Mass.: unpub., 1929.

Moxom, Philip S., *Mary Lyon Centennial and the Higher Education of Women*. Springfield, Mass.: Press of Springfield Industrial Institute [1897].

ABOUT MARY LYON'S SCHOOLS

Boas, Louise Schutz, *Women's Education Begins: The Rise of the Women's Colleges*. Norton, Mass.: Wheaton College Press, 1935.

Caldwell, Lydia Anne, *Our Honored Seminary, 1828-April 23, 1903*. Ipswich, Mass.: unpub., 1903.

Cole, Arthur C., *A Hundred Years of Mount Holyoke College: The Evolution of an Educational Ideal*. New Haven: Yale University Press, 1940.

Larcom, Lucy, *Wheaton Seminary: A Semi-Centennial Sketch*. Cambridge, Mass.: The Riverside Press, 1885.

Shepard, Grace F., *Reference History of Wheaton College*. Norton, Mass.: unpub., 1931.

Stowe, Sarah D., *History of Mount Holyoke Seminary, South Hadley, Massachusetts During Its First Half Century, 1837-1887*. South Hadley: Pub. by the Seminary, 1887.

Warner, Frances Lester, *On a New England Campus*. Boston: Houghton Mifflin Co., 1937.

Woody, Thomas, *History of Women's Education in the United States, Vol. I*. New York: Science Press, 1929.

ABOUT MARY LYON'S TIMES

Beecher, Catherine, *Educational Reminiscences and Suggestions*. New York: Harper & Brothers, 1874.

Bowne, Eliza S., *A Girl's Life Eighty Years Ago*. New York: Charles Scribner's Sons, 1887.

SELECTED LIST OF AUTHORITIES

Clark, George Faber, *A History of the Town of Norton*. Boston: Crosby, Nichols and Co., 1859.

Davis, Emerson, *The Half Century*. Boston: Tappan and Whittemore, 1851.

Eastman, Sophie E., *In Old South Hadley*. Chicago: Blakely Printing Co., 1912.

Ewell, John Lewis, *Story of Byfield: A New England Parish*. Boston: George E. Littlefield, 1904.

Felt, Joseph B., *The Customs of New England*. Boston: Press of T. R. Marvin, 1853.

Felt, Joseph B., *The History of Ipswich, Essex, and Hamilton*. Cambridge, Mass.: Charles Folsom, 1834.

Hall, S. R. and Baker, A. R., *School History of the United States*. Andover, Mass.: William Peirce, 1839.

Howes, Frederick G., *History of the Town of Ashfield, Franklin County, Massachusetts from its Settlement in 1742 to 1910*. Ashfield, Mass.: Town of Ashfield, n.d.

Hunt, Gaillard, *Life in America One Hundred Years Ago*. New York: Harper and Brothers, 1914.

Johnson, Clifton, *Old-Time Schools and Schoolbooks*. New York: Macmillan and Co., 1904.

Kendrick, Francis Shaw, *The History of Buckland (1779-1935)*. Rutland, Vermont: Tuttle Publishing Co. Inc., 1937.

McAllister, Ethel M., *Amos Eaton, Scientist and Educator, 1776-1842*. Philadelphia: University of Pennsylvania Press, 1941.

Parker, Edward L., *The History of Londonderry*. Boston: Perkins and Whipple, 1851.

Small, Walter H., *Early New England Schools*. Boston: Ginn and Co., 1914.